Skills for **Employability**

Step UP

B1+

Coursebook and **eBook**

Lynn Bonesteel
Robyn Brinks Lockwood
Carolyn Mailler
Azra Uslu

Step Up B1+

Pearson Education, 221 River Street, Hoboken, NJ 07030 USA

Cover Illustration: Roy Hermelin

Text composition: Straive

Library of Congress Cataloging-in-Publication Data: A catalog record for the print edition is available from the Library of Congress.

Printed in the United States of America

ISBN-13: 978-0-13-747360-1

1 2023

Acknowledgments

We would like to thank the following people for their help with this project.

Güzide Göksen Birol, Istanbul Okan University; **Eduardo Pinell Campuzano,** CIU Director, Universidad Privada Franz Tamayo; **Meg Cassamally,** University of Siena; **Adrian Crawley,** Evority Learning Centre; University of Siena; **Yabancı Diller,** School of Foreign Languages; **Louise Dixon,** Director of Studies at Hallo! Servizi Linguistici; **Aybala Eren,** Gazi University; **Alex Fayle,** Well & Will Language Academy; **Elizabeth Cruz Flores,** Tecnológico de Monterrey; **Jacques Friggieri,** Redrob; **María Amparo Garcia,** ICPNA Cusco; **Christina Gebbia,** Director of Let's Talk English Center in Valencia; **Maria de la Paz Giglio,** New Concept School of English; **Zeynep Güler,** İstanbul Okan University; **Ilaria Incorvaia,** ITIS 'Antonio Meucci', Florence; **Nancy Johnstone,** School of Engineering, UBA, Buenos Aires, Argentina; **Sevil Altıkulaçoğlu Kayaer,** Gazi University; **Yeliz Korkmaz,** Yıldız Technical University, Turkey; **Héctor Raúl Sánchez Lozano,** Proulex Universidad de Guadalajara; **Mariana Juana Aviles Martillo,** coordinator of CEFI, Center for Continuing Educatiòn and Interamerican Labor; **Anne Marie Mc Gowan,** University of Rome 'Tor Vergata' Italy; **Cristian Meléndez,** Universidad Católica de El Salvador; **Jose Manuel Mendivil S.,** Centro Boliviano Americano - Fundación Cultural y Educativa La Paz; **Paul Cruz Montenegro,** English Coordinator of CRC - Peru Cruceros; **M.Àngels Nogué,** Centre D'Idiomes Olot; **Irem Ozcan,** Gazi University, College of Foreign Languages; **Claudia Posarelli,** ITIS Meucci Firenze; **Steven Pragnell,** Astex Servicios Lingüísticos, Madrid; **María de Lourdes Camarillo Rodríguez,** Escuela Bancaria y Comercial; **Raquel Sánchez,** Faculty of Education in Albacete (UCLM); **Chayapak Tangapiwut,** Burapha University Language Institute; **Onur Uludag,** Yildiz Technical University; **Taku Umeda,** Tokyo Business and Language College; **Laura Vacca,** Inglese su Misura; **Marijke van Leuven,** Oxford School of English, Verona, Italy.

Photo Credits Page 2 (1): Shutterstock; 2 (2) Shutterstock; 2 (3) DGLimages/Shutterstock; 2 (4): Undrey/Shutterstock; 2 (5) Barock/Shutterstock; 2 (6) Shutterstock Air Images/Shutterstock; 5: Antonio Guillem/123RF; 6: Fizkes/Shutterstock; 7: Fizkes/Shutterstock; 8: Cartoon Resource/Shutterstock; 9: Wee dezign/Shutterstock; 10: Prostock-studio/Shutterstock; 11: Stock-Asso/Shutterstock; 12: Trueffelpix/Shutterstock; 13: Michaelheim/Shutterstock; 14 (Simon): Drazen Zigic/Shutterstock; 14 (Andrea): Standret/Shutterstock; 16 (Peggy Whitson): Courtesy of NASA; 16 (The Beatles): AP/Shutterstock; 16 (Malala Yousafzai): Entertainment Pictures/Alamy Stock Photo; 17: Party people studio/Shutterstock; 18: GaudiLab/Shutterstock; 19 (1): Fizkes/Shutterstock; 19 (2): Fizkes/Shutterstock; 19 (3): Rawpixel.com/Shutterstock; 19 (4): Stylephotographs/123RF; 19 (5): Pixel-Shot/Shutterstock; 20 (horse): Hennadii H/Shutterstock; 20 (dog): Pretty Vectors/Shutterstock; 20 (chickens): Eloku/Shutterstock; 20 (eagle): Tomacco/Shutterstock; 21: Gorodenkoff/Shutterstock; 22 (1): Branislav Nenin/Shutterstock; 22 (2): Dean Drobot/Shutterstock; 22 (3): Art_Photo/Shutterstock; 25: Shutterstock; 26: Ground Picture/Shutterstock; 27: BearFotos/Shutterstock; 28: Colorlife/Shutterstock; 29 (top): Leszek Czerwonka/Shutterstock; 29 (bottom): Jack Frog/Shutterstock; 30 (Jason): Prostock-studio/Shutterstock; 30 (Zola): Drazen Zigic/Shutterstock; 30 (Kane): Prathankarnpap/Shutterstock; 32 (Beth): Fizkes/Shutterstock; 32 (Feng): Chaay_Tee/Shutterstock; 32 (Hector): Chaay_Tee/Shutterstock; 32 (Nia): Fizkes/Shutterstock; 33: Lucky Business/Shutterstock; 34 (Chad Wilson): FamVeld/Shutterstock; 34 (social media icons): Rashad Ashur/Shutterstock; 34 (email icons): WonderfulPixel/Shutterstock; 34 (Cynthia Chen): Chaay_Tee/Shutterstock; 34 (social media icons): Rashad Ashur/Shutterstock; 34 (email icons): WonderfulPixel/Shutterstock; 35 (Sean Gordon): Billion Photos/Shutterstock; 34 (social media icons): Rashad Ashur/Shutterstock; 34 (email icons): WonderfulPixel/Shutterstock; 36 (weights): Ssstocker/123RF; 36 (laptop): Antlii/Shutterstock; 36 (camera): Antlii/Shutterstock; 36 (film): Antlii/Shutterstock; 36 (stretching): Macrovector/123RF; 36 (sitting at desk): Macrovector/123RF; 36 (tennis): Macrovector/123RF; 36 (tea): SuperHUI/Shutterstock; 36 (sneaker): Ku_suriuri/Shutterstock; 37: Ground Picture/Shutterstock; 38 (Business 1): Aleksei Kochev/Shutterstock; 38 (Business 2): Joe Mercier/Shutterstock; 39: Kukiat B/Shutterstock; 40 (box): Vertes Edmond mihai/123RF; 40 (store): PhoelixDE/Shutterstock; 40 (car): Graphicbee/123RF; 40 (stack of paper): Zern Liew/Shutterstock; 40 (monitors): Antlii/Shutterstock; 40 (houseplant): SuperHUI/Shutterstock; 40 (compost): Akinina/123RF; 40 (trophy): Macrovector/123RF; 41: Pressmaster/Shutterstock; 42: Kateryna Onyshchuk/Shutterstock; 44: Lemberg Vector studio/Shutterstock; 45: GaudiLab/Shutterstock; 46 (Interview 1): Stock 4you/Shutterstock; 46 (Interview 2): AJR_photo/Shutterstock; 46 (Interview 3): Dean Drobot/Shutterstock; 47 (Camila): Stock 4you/Shutterstock; 47 (Taner): AJR_photo/Shutterstock; 47 (Paige): Dean Drobot/Shutterstock; 48 (left): Bsd studio/Shutterstock; 48 (center left): Bsd studio/Shutterstock; 48 (center): Bsd studio/Shutterstock; 48 (center right): Bsd studio/Shutterstock; 48 (right): Bsd studio/Shutterstock; 49: Luckybusiness/123RF; 50: Production Perig/Shutterstock; 52 (man with headphones): Vadym Pastukh/Shutterstock; 52 (mask and capes): LightField Studios/Shutterstock; 52 (gnome): Anela.k/Shutterstock; 73 (woman and man avatars): Gurza/Shutterstock; 75 (woman and man avatars): Gurza/Shutterstock; 77 (woman and man avatars): Gurza/Shutterstock; 79 (woman and man avatars): Gurza/Shutterstock; 80 (woman avatar): Gurza/Shutterstock; 81 (woman and man avatars): Gurza/Shutterstock; 83 (woman and man avatars): Gurza/Shutterstock.

Scope and Sequence

Pronunciation	Language Strategy	Project	Talk!
The letter *o*	Recognize definitions	Interview people about a workplace conflict they had and then resolved	Rate five common workplace conflicts
The vowels /i/ and /ɪ/	Organize your ideas	Research communication problems and effective tips online	Reasons leading to miscommunication at work
Stressed syllables	Identify comparisons	Make a questionnaire and interview people who achieved a personal goal	Successful people who achieved their goals
The sound /ʃ/	Summarize	Research a common team problem and suggest a solution	Different types of team players
Consonant groups	Infer a writer's purpose	Find and explain why a source is reliable	Ways to verify online information
The sound /ər/	Recognize a speaker's attitude	Interview people about leaders they have worked with	Facts about how to achieve effective leadership

Module	I can . . .	Learning Objectives	Vocabulary
7 **Self-Management** Time-Management Strategies Pages 29–32	I can explain time-management strategies related to procrastination.	• Explain what procrastination is and why it is a problem • Describe the common reasons people procrastinate • Identify strategies to overcome procrastination	*accomplishment, appealing, complex, distract, have a handle on, incentive, overcome, overwhelming, prioritize, rank, rewarding, workload*
8 **Wellness** Managing Stress pages 33–36	I can explain how to manage stress.	• Identify three common types of things that cause stress • Explain how stress affects us • Describe ways to manage stress	*address, anxious, commit to, get rid of, grateful, nausea, pressure, psychological, recognize, relaxation*
9 **Social Responsibility** Business Sustainability pages 37–40	I can explain what business sustainability is.	• Explain how business sustainability relates to the planet, people, and profit • Describe things companies can do to improve business sustainability	*abuse, assess, disposal, diversity, emission, investment, manufacturer, practice, pursue, value*
10 **Branding** Creating a Career Portfolio pages 41–44	I can explain how to create a career portfolio.	• Explain the purpose of a career portfolio • Describe the components of a career portfolio • Explain two ways to prepare a career portfolio for sharing	*certification, contribution, evaluation, highlight, overview, relate, résumé, stand out, summarize, supervise, trait, transcript*
11 **Job Search** The Information Interview pages 45–48	I can explain how to have an informational interview.	• Describe the purpose of an informational interview • Explain how to have a successful informational interview	*advance, awkward, candidate, conduct, criticize, downside, entry-level, first-hand, good fit, impression, potential, trend*
12 **Interviewing** The Interview pages 49–52	I can explain how to prepare for a good job interview.	• Describe the eight most common types of interview questions • Explain how to respond appropriately to interview questions	*anticipate, applicant, characteristic, circumstance, excel, face, former, productive, rejection, sell yourself, shortcoming*

Pronunciation	Language Strategy	Project	Talk!
Silent letters	Listen for enumeration	Keep track of your own procrastination	Procrastination stories
Can and *can't*	Name topics and subtopics	Create a survey and interview people about managing stress	Rank activities to help manage stress
Blending: *want to* and *have to*	Define key terms	Interview people about their employer's sustainability practices	Tips to help you and your company be more sustainable
The vowel sound /ʌ/	Recognize important information	Search for a job online and prepare three pieces of a career portfolio	The benefits of a career portfolio
Sounds and spelling: the vowels /aɪ/, /ɪ/ and /i/	Preview a text	Write questions for an informational interview	Facts about job hunting
The sounds /u/, /ʊ/, and /ʌ/	Make inferences	Research a job online, find key words, and answer the most common interview questions	Ten unusual interview questions

To the Teacher

Overview

Step Up is a flexible online course designed for adults or young adults who want to improve their employability skills—whether to get a first job, secure a promotion, find a different job, re-enter the workforce after an absence, or change fields. Although the emphasis of the course is on employability skills, *Step Up* also develops English language skills by providing vocabulary instruction and practice, listening, reading, and notetaking skills, pronunciation practice, and discussion strategies.

Levels

There are six levels of *Step Up*, CEFR A2+ to C1, Global Scale of English (GSE) 34 to 84.

***Step Up* level**	**GSE**
Step Up A2+	34–43
Step Up B1	41–51
Step Up B1+	49–58
Step Up B2	56–66
Step Up B2+	64–75
Step Up C1	73–84

Two Versions of *Step Up*

Students can study the *Step Up* course in two ways: as a self-study course or as a self-study plus course, which is the self-study course combined with a teacher-led class. As a self-study course, each level of *Step Up* takes students 18 hours to complete, though this may vary as it is self-paced. The teacher-led course provides 14 hours of class time, with additional resources and extension activities available in the Teaching Notes, which would extend class time.

Student's Components

	Self-study course	**Self-study plus course**
Online Course	✓	✓
Coursebook + eBook or eBook only	✗	✓
Resources (online)	✓	✓

Teacher's Components

	Self-study plus course
Coursebook and/or eBook	✓
Access to the Online Course	✓
Teaching Notes	✓
Resources (online)	✓

The Online Course

Students study the following 12 modules, of which the first nine are personal and social capabilities and the last three are job-seeking skills:

Module 1 Communication 1	**Module 2** Communication 2	**Module 3** Goal Setting
Module 4 Teamwork	**Module 5** Critical Thinking	**Module 6** Leadership
Module 7 Self-Management	**Module 8** Wellness	**Module 9** Social Responsibility
Module 10 Branding	**Module 11** Job Search	**Module 12** Interviewing

Each module has an employability skills coach—an animated character—who takes the students through the 10 steps of the module. Step 11 is a progress check; it includes a practice test and a graded test. If the student scores at least 70% on every graded test, they are given access to the final exam. If they score at least 80% on this assessment, they receive a certificate of completion.

For a closer look at the online course, please see the Online Module Walkthrough in the Teacher Resources.

Coursebook/eBook

The Coursebook/eBook is made up of two main sections: the modules and the back matter.

The Modules

Welcome module

The Coursebook begins with a Welcome module, which is comprised of four sections to:

- help students get to know each other and form a community of learners
- provide students with useful language they need to work effectively in class
- help students navigate the Coursebook so they get the most out of it
- introduce students to the 12 employability skills coaches they meet in the online course.

The 12 Employability Skills Modules

Following the Welcome module are the 12 employability skills modules, corresponding to each module in the online course. Students need to do each online module before they come to class. In class, you guide them through each module to reinforce what they have learned online, to deepen their understanding of the material, and to share how they can apply what they have learned to their own lives.

Back Matter

There are four sections in the back of the Coursebook and eBook:

- *Check your understanding* enables students to demonstrate they have understood the material they have studied online and gives them an opportunity to clear up any misunderstandings at the beginning of a class.
- *Discussion strategies* provide students with four different sets of strategies that can help them engage in class. These include how to work with others; clarify what you hear or clarify what you say; get and stay involved in the discussion; and organize your ideas. Audio models enable students to practice their pronunciation.
- *Vocabulary practice* gives students additional practice with the vocabulary they have learned in the online course. The first activity is a word puzzle, and the second activity uses the target words from the puzzle in context. The answers are provided in the eBook and in the Resources folder.
- *The Glossary* provides the definitions of some words or phrases printed in light brown in the Coursebook to facilitate understanding.

Flexibility

While the sequence of the modules is fixed in the coursebook, you can change the sequence to meet the needs of your students. You may want to have the class review the scope and sequence and vote on which modules to do first. If you change the sequence, we suggest you create a syllabus and upload it to the platform.

Resources for Students

All audio and video files for the online course and all audio files for the coursebook are accessible within the activities in the course. In addition, these audio and video files are also available in the Resources, to allow students to watch or listen whenever they wish without going to the lesson itself. Also included in the Resources are the reading texts, as well as answer keys to the *Vocabulary practice* in the Coursebook.

Resources for Teachers

Teaching Notes

There are general teaching notes to help you get the most out of the course. Then there are notes for each module that begin with an overview of the online module that synopsizes what the students have learned online. Following the overview are teaching notes for each step in the coursebook, including tips, extensions, culture notes, and more.

Module Walkthrough

There is also a module walkthrough that visually describes a module and the underlying pedagogy for both the online course and the coursebook.

Platform Support

To help you navigate the platform and use all the tools available, there is a guided tour when you first log on to Pearson English Connect. In addition, you will find numerous resources under the "Help" button to orient you to the platform. And to get in touch with support, you can click on Help>Documentation>Contact Support.

Welcome

① In the classroom

A Get to know your classmates

Talk to your classmates. Find someone who matches each prompt. Write their first name on the line.

Find someone who...

- loves to read ___________
- enjoys cooking ___________
- has a pet ___________
- is great at math ___________
- has ridden a motorcycle ___________
- has travelled to another country ___________

B Useful language

Complete the conversations with sentences from the box. Then listen and check your answers.

a ~~Can you repeat the instructions?~~	**d** How do you pronounce this word?
b What's the difference between "advice" and "advise"?	**e** what's the English word for "barato"?
c you're saying we should do this for homework?	**f** Could you explain that a bit more?

C Role play

PAIRS **Choose a conversation from 1B and role play it. Use different information.**

② Learn about your book

1 How many modules are in the course?

a 5 **b** 9 **c** 11 **d** 12

2 How many steps are in each module?

a 6 **b** 7 **c** 8 **d** 9

3 Look at this icon on page 5. It tells you to go to page 68. Read what is on that page. How can you use that information?

DISCUSSION STRATEGIES

Go to page 68.

____

4 On page 5, Exercise C says Check your understanding. Go to page 54. What is on that page?

a questions to test vocabulary
b questions to ask my teacher
c questions to review the Online Course
d questions to ask my partner

5 Look through Module 1. Which Steps in the book refer to Steps in the Online Course?

a Steps 1, 2, and 3
b Steps 2, 5, and 7
c Steps 3, 4, and 6
d Steps 5, 6, and 7

6 Look at the I-can statement after Step 7 in each module, for example

I can identify successful communication skills. ☐

What is it for?

____

7 What will you find on pages 72–83?

a listening practice
b grammar practice
c vocabulary practice
d pronunciation practice

8 What will you find on pages 86–87?

a a glossary
b listening activities
c vocabulary practice
d an audio script

To find the answers for CHECK YOUR UNDERSTANDING and VOCABULARY PRACTICE you can look in your ebook or use the answer key in the Student's Resources online.

Meet your Employability Skills Coaches

MODULE 1
Greetings! I'm Dr. Jabu Cele. I have my doctorate in communications and I'm a senior vice president at one of the world's top marketing companies.

MODULE 2
Hi there! I'm Emma Lu, and I'll be your coach for the Communication 2 module. I'm a corporate teamwork coach.

MODULE 3
Hello there. I'm Zehra Teke and I'll be your Employability Skills coach for the module about Goal Setting. I'm a business consultant with a master's degree in management.

MODULE 4
Hello! My name is Kristine Ross. I'm the human resources manager for a large, international company. I'll be your coach for the Teamwork module.

MODULE 5
Hello. My name is Marek Kamiński. I'm an investigative journalist and I'll be your Employability Skills coach for the Critical Thinking module.

MODULE 6
Hi, I'm Sonia Lopez. I'll be your coach for the Leadership module. I'm the Chief Executive Officer—the CEO—of the Alacarte Restaurant Group.

MODULE 7
Hello, my name is Felix Becker. I'm a professional certified life coach and I'll be your coach for the Self-Management module.

MODULE 8
Hello and welcome to the Wellness module. I'll be your Employability Skills coach. My name is Kai Sugimoto. I have a PhD in psychology and I do research on health and wellness.

MODULE 9
Hello, there. My name is Ana Silva. I'm the coordinator of social responsibilty for a large company and I am your coach for the Social Responsibilty module.

MODULE 10
Hi. Welcome to the Branding module. I'm Rakesh Patel, and I'm your Employability Skills coach. I work in marketing.

MODULE 11
Hello! Welcome. I'm Justin Roy, and I'm your coach for the Job Search module. I'm a career advice blogger and my goal is to help people find their dream jobs.

MODULE 12
Hi. My name is Aisha Omar. I'm a career counselor at the U.S. Department of Labor and I'll be your coach for the Interviewing module.

1

MODULE

Communication 1

Resolving Conflict

DISCUSSION STRATEGIES

Go to page 68.

Step 1 Get started

A Refresh your memory! Watch the *What You'll Learn* video.

B Look at the photo. What advice could you give the two people to help them manage their conflict?

C Check your understanding. Go to page 54.

Step 2 Tell your story

A THINK In your online course, you thought about a time you resolved a conflict at work, school, or in your personal life. What happened, and what did you learn? Listen to the example.

B PAIRS Discuss your story.

C SHARE Tell your story to the class.

Step 3 Activate your knowledge

A PAIRS Read the situation. Then listen to two versions of a conversation between Lucas and Paul. What is the conflict?

Situation

Lucas and Paul are coworkers at an insurance company. Lucas has worked there for several years. Paul has been there for two months. When Paul was hired, Lucas's supervisor asked him to help Paul out.

The conflict is ______________________________.

B SHARE Listen again. Analyze how Paul and Lucas communicated. What did they do right or wrong in each conversation? Take notes in the charts.

CONVERSATION 1
Examples of good communication:
Examples of bad communication:

CONVERSATION 2

Examples of good communication:

Examples of bad communication:

C PAIRS Which conversation is more successful at resolving the conflict? Explain.

D SHARE Present your answers to **C** to the class. Add notes to the chart while other pairs share their answers.

Step 4 Take away

GROUPS of 3–5 Complete the chart. Write the conflict resolution tips from your answers to Step 3, the ones you learned from your classmates, and any others you learned in the course.

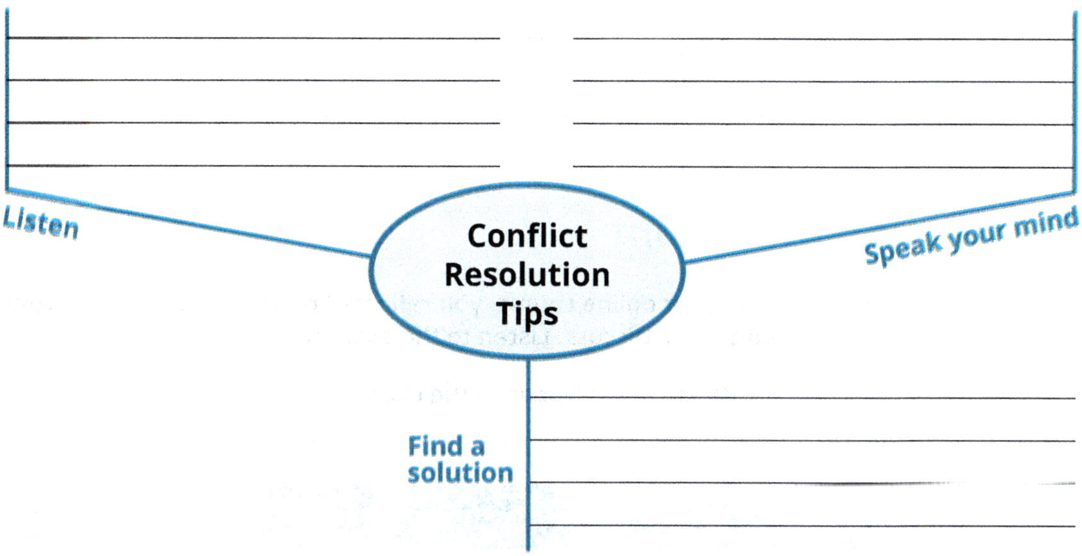

Step 5 Project

PAIRS **In your online course, you interviewed one to two people who had a workplace conflict and resolved it successfully. Discuss how the conflicts were resolved. Did the people use any of the suggestions from the module? Which ones? Read the example.**

I interviewed my brother about a conflict he had at work. He's a paralegal and he missed an important deadline. The lawyer he was working for was concerned, but she didn't yell at my brother or get upset. She used "I" messages so that my brother didn't get defensive. Instead, he took responsibility and apologized. They discussed why it happened and thought of a plan to make sure it didn't happen again.

I think the conflict was resolved for several reasons. First, the lawyer remained calm and used "I" messages instead of making accusations. Second, my brother took responsibility for his mistake and apologized. Finally, they brainstormed and found a solution to prevent it from happening again.

Step 6 Talk!

GROUPS of 3–4 **Conflicts will always occur in the workplace. Here are five common workplace conflicts. Rate them from 1–5, from the least serious to the most serious. Compare your responses. Talk about why you rated the conflicts the way you did.**

Workplace Conflicts
- ☐ poor communication
- ☐ personality differences
- ☐ irritating behaviors
- ☐ unclear or poor management
- ☐ unfair treatment

Think of another conflict. Discuss why you added it and how serious you think it is.

____

____

Step 7 Going forward

A **PAIRS** **In your online course, you reflected on how you could improve your conflict resolution skills. Discuss. Listen to the example.**

B **SHARE** **Present your ideas to the class.**

VOCABULARY PRACTICE
Go to page 74.

I can describe specific strategies for managing and resolving conflict. ☐

2

MODULE

Communication 2

Handling Miscommunication

DISCUSSION STRATEGIES

Go to page 68.

Step 1

Get started

A Refresh your memory! Watch the *What You'll Learn* video.

B Look at the photo. Think about this workplace interaction. Describe the situation.

C Check your understanding. Go to page 55.

Step 2 Tell your story

A THINK **In your online course, you thought about a time you miscommunicated at work, school, or in your personal life. What happened, and what did you learn? Listen to the example.**

B PAIRS **Discuss your story.**

C SHARE **Tell your story to the class.**

Step 3 Activate your knowledge

A PAIRS **Read the scenarios. Discuss the miscommunications and then answer the questions. Take notes.**

1

Marco received an email invitation from the HR department of his company to an online training session that all employees had to attend. He took part in the training but had to leave five minutes early to rush to another meeting with a customer. The next day, he got an angry call from Alex, his manager, accusing him of not attending the training and demanding to know why. Marco calmly explained the situation, but Alex still was not happy. "You're talking about the first training session. There was a second one 30 minutes later. And you weren't there!" Marco was surprised but remained calm and explained that the email invitation only mentioned one training session and that he did not realize there was another one.

- **What communication mistake did Alex make?**

____

____

____

- **What communication mistake did Marco make?**

____

____

____

- **How should they resolve the problem?**

____

____

____

2 Tanya had a habit of copying everyone in the department on all the emails she sent out, just to make sure she did not miss anyone important. Several people complained about getting emails that had nothing to do with them. Since then, Tanya has been more careful about who she copies on emails. If she is not sure, she asks her boss.

- **What communication mistake did Tanya make?**

___

___

___

- **How did Tanya fix her mistake?**

___

___

___

B PAIRS **Review scenario 1. Write a role play in which Marco and Alex resolve the miscommunication. One student takes the role of Alex, and the other takes the role of Marco.**

Alex: ___

Marco: ___

Alex: ___

Marco: ___

C GROUPS of 4–6 **Perform your role plays. Then compare the different ways you and your classmates chose to handle the miscommunication. Discuss the different solutions.**

Step 4 Take away

A PAIRS **Complete the chart with the words and phrases in the box.**

apologize	use passive language	be calm	clarify	make excuses	take responsibility

Dos	Don'ts

B SHARE **Compare your answers with another pair's. Think of other tips that you can add to the chart.**

Step 5 Project

PAIRS In your online course, you researched communication problems at work. You found effective tips for fixing miscommunication that were not discussed in the podcast. Share your tips with the class. Read the example.

One source of miscommunication at work is that people don't always answer questions respectfully, especially in emails. You might be tempted to shoot off a one- or two-word reply, but it makes it sound rude and abrupt. Even if your email answers the question, it may create bad feelings between coworkers. And that can lead to even more communication problems.

A tip for fixing email miscommunication is to pick up the phone and call the person instead of going back and forth by email. It is difficult to communicate tone in an email. Sometimes the best way to fix a misunderstanding is to talk to the person directly.

Step 6 Talk!

GROUPS of 3–5 Now let's think about five common reasons leading to miscommunication at work. Then discuss the questions below.

Five common reasons for miscommunication at work

Using the wrong medium

Poor listening/ speaking skills

Lack of context

Giving too much/too little information

Ambiguity

- Which reason do you think is the most common one? Why?
- How can these reasons lead to miscommunication in the workplace? Describe.
- How can these miscommunications be fixed?

Step 7 Going forward

A PAIRS In your online course, you reflected on how you could improve your workplace communication skills. Discuss. Listen to the example.

B SHARE Present your ideas to the class.

VOCABULARY PRACTICE
Go to page 75.

I can describe miscommunication and the strategies for resolving it at work. ☐

3

MODULE

Goal Setting

Monitoring Progress

DISCUSSION STRATEGIES

Go to page 68.

Step 1

Get started

A Refresh your memory! Watch the *What You'll Learn* video.

B Look at the photo. What goal might the person be working toward? How could she monitor her progress?

C Check your understanding. Go to page 56.

Step 2 Tell your story

A THINK **In your online course, you thought about a time you set a goal at work, school, or in your personal life. What happened, and what did you learn? Listen to the example.**

B PAIRS **Discuss your story.**

C SHARE **Tell your story to the class.**

Step 3 Activate your knowledge

A PAIRS **Read Simon's scenario. List at least three ways Simon is monitoring his progress. Take notes.**

Simon has two part-time jobs in information technology, but he would prefer to have one full-time job. His original goal was to find a job within two months, but after looking for about a month and talking to his friend, he adjusted his timeline. He has given himself three more months. With his new timeline, he began making a week-by-week plan. He records the jobs he's applied for that week and makes notes about what happened with each application. He reviews the plan and his notes every Monday morning to check the status of his job applications. Then he updates his friend on his progress and together they make a list of ideas about what else Simon might need to do to find a job. For example, based on a podcast his friend heard about job searches, Simon decided that he needed to start attending more networking events. He looked up networking events in his local area and added a few to his weekly plan.

Simon's ways to monitor progress:

____

____

____

B PAIRS **Read Andrea's scenario. Make a list of 3–5 things Andrea should do to monitor her progress.**

Andrea's goal is to open up a small café in the town where she lives. She got a loan from the bank and rented the space where the café will be. She and her brother will work in the café, so she does not need to hire anyone. The space she is renting already has most of the kitchen equipment she needs. She has six months to get the café up and running. In that time, she needs to buy furniture, dishes, and silverware, and she also has to decorate the space. She needs to find a supplier for the coffee and baked goods. She set up a page on a social media site for the café, but lately she has been too busy to post anything. She currently has about 100 followers, including family, friends, and neighbors.

Advice for Andrea:

____

____

____

C SHARE Compare your advice for Andrea with another pair's. Add their ideas to your list.

Step 4 Take away

A PAIRS Using the information from Step 3 and the online module, match the ways to monitor progress with the correct example.

Examples

a Schedule regular time and set up reminders in your calendar to reflect on your progress.

b Post updates on your progress and any changes to your plan on your blog.

c Check if the things you are doing are bringing you closer to your goal.

d Look at the points in your plan again and make sure they are realistic.

e Start a blog about your plan and share it with your family and friends.

f If what you are doing is not having the effect you want, make changes to your plan or goal—or both.

Ways to Monitor Progress

6 ______

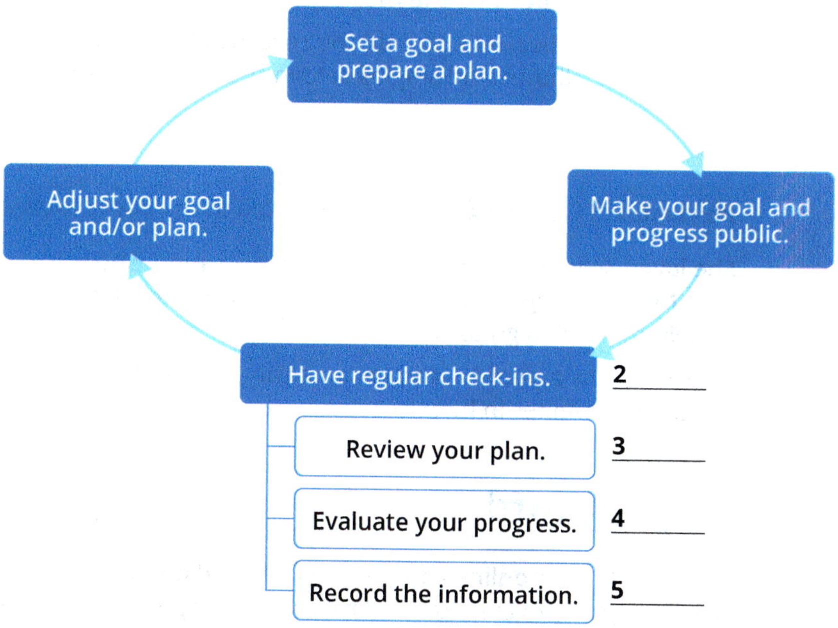

1 ______

2 ______

3 ______

4 ______

5 ______

B SHARE Check your answers with the class.

Step 5 Project

PAIRS In your online course, you interviewed people about a goal they achieved and how they monitored their progress. Share what you learned with the class. Read the example.

I interviewed a friend who saved enough money to buy a new car. She did something that I had never heard of before—she found an online support group for people who want to save money. What's really cool is that the support group follows the same strategies that we learned about! But they give you a buddy who helps you monitor your progress. If your plan isn't working, you discuss it and make changes.

Step 6 Talk!

GROUPS of 3–5 Achieving big goals takes planning and hard work but can give you international recognition. Read about these successful people who hold world records for their achievements. Think about what goes into achieving success. Then discuss.

PEGGY WHITSON: U.S. astronaut and biochemist

She decided that she wanted to become an astronaut while watching the first moon landing in 1969. She studied biology and chemistry and worked at the Johnson Space Center in Houston, Texas.

As of 2021, she holds the record for the most times a female astronaut has made a spacewalk, or gone outside the space station or vehicle in space: 10.

THE BEATLES: British rock band formed in 1960

They all grew up in Liverpool, a coastal town in England, and worked hard to become the most influential band of all time.

As of 2021, the Beatles still hold the records for the most number one albums and singles sold in the United States.

MALALA YOUSAFZAI: Pakistani women's rights activist

She loved school and wanted to get an education. She was shot for attending school in her country. She started a charity to help other girls go to school.

In 2014, at the age of 17, she became the youngest Nobel Peace Prize winner in history.

Step 7 Going forward

A PAIRS In your online course, you reflected on how you could improve your ability to monitor your progress toward reaching your goals. Discuss. Listen to the example.

B SHARE Present your ideas to the class.

VOCABULARY PRACTICE
Go to page 76.

I can describe strategies for monitoring progress in order to achieve goals. ☐

4 MODULE

Teamwork

Solving Team Problems

DISCUSSION STRATEGIES

Go to page 68.

Step 1 Get started

A Refresh your memory! Watch the *What You'll Learn* video.

B Look at the photo. What are some problems that teams often have?

C Check your understanding. Go to page 57.

Step 2 Tell your story

A THINK In your online course, you thought about a time you were on a team that had a problem. What happened, and what did you learn? Listen to the example.

B PAIRS Discuss your story.

C SHARE Tell your story to the class.

Step 3 Activate your knowledge

A PAIRS Read the scenario. Then listen to the conversation between two team members. Match the problems the team is having with the sentences from the conversation. One of the problems will not be used.

Dylan and Ada

Dylan is a graphic designer and Ada is a writer at an advertising agency. They are both working on a team that is responsible for creating a successful advertising campaign for an important new client.

Sentences

_____ 1 But during meetings with management, the other team members take all the credit.

_____ 2 I've given up trying to change things.

_____ 3 ... at the end of the meeting, it's not clear to me how the work is going to get done, or who's going to do it.

_____ 4 And the team leader doesn't set up regular check-in times between meetings, so I'm never sure where we're at in the campaign.

Problems

a unclear goals

b lack of trust

c no clear roles or responsibilities

d reduced engagement

e inadequate information sharing

B PAIRS What do you think Dylan and Ada can do to solve their team's problems? Complete the chart with the problems from A. Then write your suggestions next to each problem.

Problems	Solutions

C SHARE Discuss what you think the problems are and share your suggestions for solving them. Add your classmates' ideas to your chart.

Step 4 Take away

A PAIRS Look at the photos. Label each one with a solution to common team problems from the box and write a note on how each one contributes to a team's success. Use information from Step 3, the online module, and your own ideas.

Explicit goals	Effective information sharing	Trust building
~~Renewed engagement~~	Clear roles and responsibilities	

1 

Renewed engagement

Engaged employees are more motivated to help their team succeed. They enjoy their work and build strong relationships with co-workers.

2 

3 

4 

5 

B SHARE Compare your answers with another pair's.

Step 5 Project

PAIRS In your online course, you researched an example of a common team problem and suggested a solution. Explain how this can help you in your job or at school. Read the example.

One common team problem is when some members of a group are afraid that others will reject their ideas. So they end up not participating in team discussions. I was really interested in this problem because it happens to me all the time! But I had no idea so many other people feel the same way. One suggestion I have is for the team leader to make a rule: When someone shares an idea, the next person who speaks must say something positive about it before they criticize or give their own ideas. That way the team members stay positive and everyone feels safe speaking up.

Step 6 Talk!

PAIRS Each person brings different talents and work styles to the team. Read about these types of team members. Then discuss them using the questions below.

THE WORKHORSE Just like the workhorse, these team members focus on tasks and work very hard to accomplish them. Instead of talking about things, they prefer doing them.

THE GUIDE DOG Like trusted guide dogs, these team members focus in the goal. They are flexible and eager to help others, all while staying enthusiastic about the project.

THE MOTHER HEN Like the mother hen caring for her flock, these team members focus on the process. They ensure the project moves forward as planned and the atmosphere on the team is good.

THE EAGLE EYE Similar to the eagle that can spot tiny creatures from a great height, these team players focus on both the big picture and the details. They like to think things through first and aren't afraid to take risks.

- Do you recognize any of these team player types in yourself?
- Which types have you worked with? Which one do you enjoy working with most? The least?
- Why is it good for the team to have different types of team players?

Step 7 Going forward

A PAIRS In your online course, you reflected on how you could improve your teamwork skills. Discuss. Listen to the example.

B SHARE Present your ideas to the class.

VOCABULARY PRACTICE
Go to page 77.

I can describe ways to recognize and resolve common team problems. ☐

5
MODULE

Critical Thinking

Analyzing and Evaluating Information

DISCUSSION STRATEGIES

Go to page 68.

Step 1

Get started

A Refresh your memory! Watch the *What You'll Learn* video.

B Look at the student doing research. What advice would you give her about how to analyze and evaluate information?

C Check your understanding. Go to page 58.

Step 2 Tell your story

A THINK In your online course, you thought about a time you analyzed and evaluated information at work, school, or in your personal life. What happened, and what did you learn? Listen to the example.

B PAIRS Discuss your story.

C SHARE Tell your story to the class.

Step 3 Activate your knowledge

A PAIRS Read the scenarios and listen to the conversations. What have each of the researchers done to evaluate their sources? Take notes.

1 Alma has just started college, and she is getting ready to write her first research paper about a political figure. She wants to do a good job, but she is not confident about her ability to analyze and evaluate sources. She asks a research librarian for help in choosing reliable sources for her research.

____

____

2 Beth and David are working together on a project for a college course. Part of their grade will be based on their ability to choose good sources. They are discussing the information they've found so far and are trying to determine its reliability.

____

____

3 Omar and Hana are co-workers. Their manager wrote an article quickly for their company's website and did not analyze the sources he used for the article. He has asked Omar and Hana to check his sources for reliability before it is posted.

____

____

B PAIRS Listen again. Answer the questions.

1 To evaluate the article, what is the question Alma should ask next?

- ☐ Is the author qualified to write about this subject?
- ☐ Does the article contain misinformation?
- ☐ Does the article use extreme language?

2 To evaluate the information in the graph, what is the question Beth and David should ask next?

- ☐ Is the information from the original source objective?
- ☐ When was the website created?
- ☐ Is the company that created the website well-known?

3 To evaluate the statistics, what question should Omar and Hana ask next?

- ☐ Are we biased on the topic?
- ☐ Is the information on the website reviewed?
- ☐ What is the source of the statistics?

C SHARE Compare your answers to A and B with another pair's. Can you think of any other suggestions about how the researchers could evaluate the sources? Take notes.

Step 4 Take away

A GROUPS of 3–5 Put the questions used to analyze and evaluate information in the correct category.

1 Is the publication date provided?
2 Who is the site owner?
3 Is the information meant to be false and deceptive?
4 Does the source have a subjective point of view?
5 What is the domain name? Is it .com, .org, .edu, or .gov?
6 Is the information up-to-date or dated?
7 Is the source objective by presenting only facts?
8 Is the information reviewed?
9 Does the source use biased, one-sided arguments?

a What is the source? ______ ______ ______

b When was the information created? ______ ______

c How reliable is the information? ______ ______ ______ ______

B SHARE Check your answers with the class.

Step 5 Project

PAIRS In your online course, you found a source of information on a topic that interests you and evaluated its reliability. Explain what your topic is, what your source is, and why you think it is reliable. Read the example.

My topic is cell phone technology. My source is a website created by a well-known university, MIT, with a .edu domain name, so I was pretty sure it would be reliable. But because the technology is changing so fast, I checked the date of the posted article. Luckily, it was current. Then I read the article carefully to check for any emotional language. There wasn't any, and all the facts were supported by evidence. So I feel like it's a reliable source.

Step 6 Talk!

PAIRS The internet has made it easy to publish information quickly and share it with people around the globe. That is why a lot of it is often inaccurate. Look at some popular methods of verifying online information. Which of them do you use? Which do you think are effective? Discuss the methods.

How people worldwide analyze and evaluate online information		*Do you do this?*	*Is this effective?*
I check what other media say about the story.	**43%**	☐	☐
I find and verify the original source.	**39%**	☐	☐
I research the organization that published the story.	**32%**	☐	☐
I check whether the headline matches the story.	**27%**	☐	☐
I verify the story on a fact-checking website.	**27%**	☐	☐
I read the comments about the story.	**27%**	☐	☐
I ask family and friends if they know the story.	**21%**	☐	☐
I check the person who shared the story if it's on social media.	**16%**	☐	☐
I check how many people have shared or liked the story on social media.	**7%**	☐	☐
I do nothing to check the information.	**4%**	☐	☐

Step 7 Going forward

A PAIRS In your online course, you reflected on how you could improve your ability to analyze and evaluate information. Discuss. Listen to the example.

B SHARE Present your ideas to the class.

VOCABULARY PRACTICE
Go to page 78.

I can describe critical thinking and explain its importance in analyzing online information. ☐

6

MODULE

Leadership

How to Be a Leader

DISCUSSION STRATEGIES

Go to page 68.

Step 1 Get started

A Refresh your memory! Watch the *What You'll Learn* video.

B Look at the photo. What qualities does someone like a fire chief need to be an effective leader?

C Check your understanding. Go to page 59.

Step 2 Tell your story

A THINK In your online course, you thought about a time you were a leader at work, school, or in your personal life. What happened, and what did you learn? Listen to the example.

B PAIRS Discuss your story.

C SHARE Tell your story to the class.

Step 3 Activate your knowledge

A PAIRS Read the performance reviews. What are each person's strengths as a leader? What do they need to work on? Take notes in the charts.

1

Performance Review

Employee	Position
Jackson Simmons	*Project Manager*

Summary

Jackson has shown excellent growth as a manager over the past year. He was put in charge of three major projects, all of which were successfully completed. I knew that three projects in a year was going to be a lot, but Jackson handled things well. His teams regularly gave him high marks for keeping them engaged in the work. A large number of team members mentioned his communication skills, saying that he made them feel "heard." He struggled a bit when faced with disagreements among team members, however. This resulted in missing an important deadline on one of his projects. To Jackson's credit, however, he came to me for advice and made some necessary changes. Overall, I am extremely pleased with the results Jackson has gotten this year and the way he has dealt with new challenges.

Strengths	Areas of Improvement	Overall Evaluation	Recommendations
		☐ above expectations ☐ meets expectations ☐ below expectations	☐ training ☐ pay increase ☐ promotion ☐ other: ______

2

Performance Review

Employee	**Position**
Antonia Sousa	*Office Manager*

Summary

Antonia has been highly effective in her role as office manager. She is efficient, creative, and decisive. In the short time she has been with us, she has set up procedures to eliminate waste, resulting in a 25% savings for the department. However, some people who report to her have expressed concern that she does not include them in the decision-making process or listen to their ideas. I have spoken to Antonia about their concerns, and we discussed ways for her to win her co-workers' trust and cooperation. Antonia is a new employee and enthusiastic, and I am confident that she will use this experience as an opportunity for growth. I look forward to seeing her become an even more effective manager in the coming year.

Strengths	Areas of Improvement	Overall Evaluation	Recommendations
		☐ above expectations ☐ meets expectations ☐ below expectations	☐ training ☐ pay increase ☐ promotion ☐ other: ______

B GROUPS of 4 Compare your ideas about each leader's performance. Then together make your overall evaluations and recommendations.

C SHARE Share your recommendations with the class. Explain.

Step 4 Take away

A PAIRS Match each leadership skill with the best example.

_____ **1** Comfortable making decisions

_____ **2** Knows how to motivate others

_____ **3** Gets people to cooperate

_____ **4** Coordinates skills and tasks

_____ **5** Open to others' ideas

Examples

a Leaves some time at the end of every meeting to get suggestions from the team and then shares them with everyone.

b Frequently meets one-on-one with team members to find out if they are comfortable with their roles and the amount of responsibility they have.

c Immediately takes charge in an emergency.

d Publicly recognizes individuals and the team for excellent work.

e Deals quickly with any conflict between team members by meeting with them to resolve the issue.

B SHARE Check your answers with another pair's.

Step ⑤ Project

PAIRS **In your online course, you interviewed a few people about leaders they have worked with. Present the information you learned to your partner. Read the example.**

One of the people I interviewed told me about his new manager. He really admires what a good coordinator she is. He says it's great to finally be working with someone who knows what people are good at and uses that information to assign work tasks. It's the first place he's worked where everyone actually does their fair share of the work—and they don't complain about it.

Step ⑥ Talk!

A **PAIRS** **Effective leadership helps organizations achieve better business results. Read the facts about leadership. What do you think is the common problem? Discuss.**

58% of team leaders and managers started in their role without any leadership training.

84% of organizations say they may not find enough people to fill all leadership positions in the next five years.

83% of organizations see the need to develop leaders at every level of the company, but only **5%** really do it.

Organizations that have a leadership development program at all levels are **four times more likely** to be successful than those that offer training only to top managers.

B **GROUPS of 4** **Together think of solutions to the problem you identified in A.**

Step ⑦ Going forward

A **PAIRS** **In your online course, you reflected on how you could improve your leadership skills. Discuss. Listen to the example.**

B **SHARE** **Present your ideas to the class.**

VOCABULARY PRACTICE
Go to page 79.

I can explain how to be a good leader. ☐

7

MODULE

Self-Management

Time-Management Strategies

DISCUSSION STRATEGIES

Go to page 68.

Step 1

Get started

A Refresh your memory! Watch the *What You'll Learn* video.

B Look at the photos. A messy desk can be a sign of procrastination. Do you think it is a problem? Why or why not?

C Check your understanding. Go to page 60.

Step 2 Tell your story

A THINK In your online course, you thought about a time you procrastinated at work, school, or in your personal life. What happened, and what did you learn? Listen to the example.

B PAIRS Discuss your story.

C SHARE Tell your story to the class.

Step 3 Activate your knowledge

A PAIRS Listen to and read about three people calling in to a radio show for advice about time management and procrastination. Write the problem(s) in the chart. Then discuss what advice you could give to each caller. Complete the chart with your solutions.

1

Jason

I'm a project manager at a big company. Although I make it easy for other people to manage their work and get projects done on time, managing my own time can be incredibly stressful. My major problem is that I put off doing things that I don't like doing. And, unfortunately, that describes about 25% of the things on my to-do list. Almost every night, I wake up worrying about what I haven't done. But, by the next morning, I've convinced myself that if I start with the tasks I enjoy, and if I can accomplish something quickly, that will give me the momentum to push through the stuff I don't like so much. Well, it almost never works, and all that stuff stays on my to-do list.

2

Zola

I work from home, which I like, because I get to set my own schedule. But that isn't what really happens. I just feel like I'm always working—and I have no control over my time. There are so many distractions! My daughter needs help with her homework; the dog needs to be walked; my elderly mother calls to tell me what she needs me to pick up at the grocery store; my son texts me and tells me he needs a ride home from baseball practice. And then there are all those emails that keep popping up in my inbox, reminding me of everything I haven't done yet. I feel like I never take a break, but my to-do list just keeps getting longer and longer—and I worry all the time about losing my job.

3

Kane

I just started a new job after being at my old job for ten years. I was really excited to take on a new challenge, but now I'm afraid it's too much for me. I'm completely overwhelmed by how much there is to learn. The problem is that when I'm overwhelmed, I can't think straight. I just want to hide in a corner until I can figure things out on my own. But I can't do that forever. The work is piling up—it's so bad that I don't even know where to begin. I've started to think I should quit my job before they fire me.

Name	Problem(s)	Solutions
Jason		
Zola		
Kane		

B GROUPS of 4 Compare your advice for each caller. Add suggestions from your classmates.

C SHARE Present your solutions to the class. Discuss what you think the best solutions are and why.

Step 4 Take away

A GROUPS of 3–5 Complete the list of ways to deal with and overcome procrastination with the words from the box.

prioritize	break	confusing	big	block out	unappealing	distractions

Reasons for procrastination and how to deal with them

If the task is too...

difficult or [1]____________, then ask for help or clarification.

[2]____________, then break it down into smaller steps.

[3]____________, then give yourself a reward when you finish it.

How to overcome procrastination

- Create a plan and [4]____________ the tasks you need to get done.
- Make sure to [5]____________ time on your calendar and commit to it.
- Limit time wasters and [6]____________.
- Take a [7]____________ when you need it.

B SHARE Check your answers with the class.

Step 5 Project

PAIRS In your online course, you kept track of what tasks you avoided and why, and how you overcame your procrastination. Tell your partner about your experience and what you learned from it. Read the example.

I found out that I tend to procrastinate when I don't have a very clear plan of what I need to do. And, strangely, I tend to procrastinate less when I have a lot of things to do! It's kind of like if I have lots of things on my to-do list, I'm almost forced to make a plan and stick to it. But if there's not much on my list, I feel like I have all the time in the world—and I just waste the whole day. So, one thing I've learned is that even if I don't have much to get done, I should still make a plan.

Step 6 Talk!

PAIRS Most people procrastinate. Read the quote and then some procrastination stories. Do any of these sound like you or people you know? Then discuss the questions.

> **"Never put off till tomorrow what may be done the day after tomorrow just as well."**
> — Mark Twain

When I donate my old clothes to a charity, I like to drive them around in the trunk of my car for about a year. — Beth

I realized in college when I was a history major that I'd rather clean the bathroom, defrost the refrigerator, and pay bills than write another paper. I changed my major the next semester. — Feng

If more than 5 months go by and I haven't put away the holiday decorations, I keep them up until next year, when the holiday rolls around again. — Hector

Five years ago, I bought a book called *How to Avoid Procrastination*. I haven't gotten around to reading it yet. It's on the list. — Nia

- Does everyone procrastinate sometimes?
- When do you usually procrastinate? Why?
- Can good things happen because of procrastination? How?

Step 7 Going forward

A **PAIRS** In your online course, you reflected on how you could improve your time-management skills. Discuss. Listen to the example.

B **SHARE** Present your ideas to the class.

VOCABULARY PRACTICE Go to page 80.

I can explain time-management strategies related to procrastination. ☐

MODULE

8 Wellness

Managing Stress

DISCUSSION STRATEGIES

Go to page 68.

Step 1 Get started

A Refresh your memory! Watch the *What You'll Learn* video.

B Look at the photo. What are they doing to reduce their stress? What else could they do?

C Check your understanding. Go to page 61.

Step 2 Tell your story

A THINK In your online course, you thought about a time you were under a lot of stress at work, school, or in your personal life. What happened, and what did you learn? Listen to the example.

B PAIRS Discuss your story.

C SHARE Tell your story to the class.

Step 3 Activate your knowledge

A PAIRS Read the posts from a social media group where people share their struggles and get support from readers. Check all correct answers. Then explain each one.

1

Chad Wilson

I'm a divorced dad of a 3-year-old daughter and a 1-year-old son. My wife and I split up a couple of months ago, and I have full custody of the kids. I teach high school math, but I haven't been at this job for long, so I'm not that close to anyone at work and I don't really talk about my private life with anyone.

All day long, I work with teenagers with lots of problems of their own. Then I get home and have two small kids to take care of. I usually pick up takeout food on the way home so at least I don't have to cook. But I'm gaining weight and feel pretty unhealthy. Help!

a What kind(s) of stress is Chad having? Explain.

☐ emotional ☐ practical ☐ change-related

____

b What are the effects of his stress? Explain.

☐ physical ☐ emotional ☐ behavioral

____

2

Cynthia Chen

My family and I just moved across the country. I'm in high school, and I really didn't want to leave my friends. I've known them since we were little. We grew up together. Now I don't know anybody my age.

The school year starts in a few weeks. I know my mom and dad love me, and they really want me to be happy. They're trying to make it nice here, and they don't want to see me sad. So, I pretend that things aren't so bad. They have no idea what my life is like here. I'm very anxious about starting at a new school and making new friends. I haven't been sleeping well. I really hope someone here can give me some advice.

a What kind(s) of stress is Cynthia having? Explain.

☐ emotional ☐ practical ☐ change-related

____

b What are the effects of her stress? Explain.

☐ physical ☐ emotional ☐ behavioral

____

3

Sean Gordon

Hey there, folks! You've helped me before, so I'm back! This time my problems are work-related. One of my co-workers just quit, and it's going to take a while to replace her.

That means I'm doing both my job AND hers. The amount of work is overwhelming, but my boss doesn't seem to notice. To make things worse, instead of working harder, I'm goofing off! I keep putting off my work and am spending lots of time looking at my smartphone. I've never had this problem before—I've always been a hard worker. Any thoughts or advice? Thanks in advance!

a What kind(s) of stress is Sean having? Explain.

☐ emotional ☐ practical ☐ change-related

____

b What are the effects of his stress? Explain.

☐ physical ☐ emotional ☐ behavioral

____

B GROUPS of 4 **Work with your classmates to think of advice for Chad, Cynthia, and Sean on how to manage their stress. Write your suggestions.**

Chad ______________________________

Cynthia ______________________________

Sean ______________________________

C SHARE **Present your suggestions to the class. Discuss.**

Step 4 Take away

GROUPS of 3–5 **Match the causes, effects, and ways of managing stress with the examples.**

Causes	Effects	Ways of managing stress
____ 1 Emotional ____ 2 Practical ____ 3 Change-related	____ 4 Physical ____ 5 Emotional ____ 6 Behavioral	____ 7 Self-care ____ 8 Organization

Examples

a Recently, Derek has stopped taking care of his appearance.
b Leo has set up reminders on his phone to make sure that he is always on time.
c Alex has gotten a dog and is taking him for long walks every day.
d Ana just graduated from college with over $50,000 in student loans.
e Stella believes she should be a director of the company by the time she is 30 years old.
f Kamal's elderly parents have just moved in with him.
g Juan suffers from very bad headaches.
h Lately, Sam finds himself crying a lot.

Step 5 Project

PAIRS In your online course, you created a survey and interviewed 2–3 people about what caused them stress and how they handled it. Tell your partner about their answers and what you learned from them. Read the example.

The three people I interviewed had similar causes of stress—pressures at home and at work. One person also had serious financial problems. Their ways of dealing with stress varied a lot. One person wasn't really doing anything—he said that he hadn't really realized how stressed he was until he talked to me! Another person went out dancing once a week to relieve her stress. And the other person was meeting with a financial coach to help her organize her finances. Doing these interviews helped me recognize how common stress is and how important it is to find effective ways of dealing with it.

Step 6 Talk!

GROUPS of 3–5 People have different ways of managing stress. Read these activities and rank them from most (10) to least (1) effective for you. Add your own ideas if they are not on the list. Then discuss your choices.

____ Go to the gym three times a week.	____ Call a friend who makes you laugh.
____ Start each day by making a to-do list.	____ Tidy up your desk at the end of each day.
____ Start a new hobby.	____ Relax by doing nothing.
____ Take a break and do breathing exercises.	____ Play games with family or friends.
____ Plan a night out with friends.	____ Go for a walk in the woods.

Step 7 Going forward

A PAIRS In your online course, you reflected on what you have learned about managing stress and how you could improve the way you manage it. Listen to the example.

B SHARE Present your ideas to the class.

VOCABULARY PRACTICE
Go to page 81.

I can explain how to manage stress. ☐

9

MODULE

Social Responsibility

Business Sustainability

DISCUSSION STRATEGIES

Go to page 68.

Step 1

Get started

A Refresh your memory! Watch the *What You'll Learn* video.

B Look at the photo. What sustainability practice does it illustrate? Explain.

C Check your understanding. Go to page 62.

Step 2 Tell your story

A THINK In your online course, you thought about a time you supported or wanted to support a sustainable practice at work, school, or in your personal life. What happened, and what did you learn? Listen to the example.

B PAIRS Discuss your story.

C SHARE Tell your story to the class.

Step 3 Activate your knowledge

A PAIRS Read the descriptions of three businesses and discuss their sustainability practices. What are their strengths and weaknesses? Take notes.

BUSINESS 1

ABC Tech is an international corporation with offices all over the world. It is committed to equal opportunity hiring practices, and it has received recognition for its diversity and family-friendly policies, including free childcare for all employees. All the company's offices have been built using environmentally-friendly materials and the latest low-carbon technology.

Recently, however, ABC Tech received some bad publicity when a reporter discovered that one of its major suppliers was using child labor. Since then, the company has had trouble finding new investors, and sales have fallen.

Strengths	
Weaknesses	

BUSINESS 2

Dalton University is a large university that was started 75 years ago. Many of the buildings are old and have not been updated. However, all university vehicles, including buses, are electric. To encourage their use, university employees and students receive a 50% discount on public transportation passes. There is very limited parking available on campus, and it is quite expensive. So, there are bike paths throughout the campus and many bike racks.

In terms of the university's faculty, about 60% of them come from North America and are from many different racial and ethnic backgrounds. The other 40% come from other regions of the world. About 80% of the faculty is male, 20% female and about 2% are disabled.

Strengths	
Weaknesses	

BUSINESS 3

Sunny Farms is a medium-sized agricultural company. It is one of the most successful fruit growers in the country making a healthy profit every year. The aim at Sunny Farms is to follow the best practices in the agricultural industry. It put a lot of money into clean energy sources, including wind and solar, and has received the highest rating from environmental groups that check the farming industry. On the other hand, most of its workers are seasonal laborers who are paid minimum wage and typically work 7 days a week, in 12-hour shifts.

Strengths	
Weaknesses	

B GROUPS Discuss each business and make suggestions for how they could improve their sustainability practices.

Business 1 ____________________

Business 2 ____________________

Business 3 ____________________

C SHARE Present your suggestions to the class.

Step 4 Take away

PAIRS Complete the chart with information from Step 3 and the online module.

bikes	diversity	expenses	gender	wind power	sales	race

Business Sustainability

Planet
- slow climate change
  - For example:
    - solar and ____________
    - ____________ and public transport
    - reduce carbon emmissions

People
- treatment of workers
- ____________
  - For example:
    - ____________
    - ethnicity
    - ____________

Profit
- increased ____________
- increased investment
- lower ____________

Step 5 Project

PAIRS In your online course, you interviewed 3-4 people who work for different companies. You asked them whether they cared about sustainability, and what their employers' sustainability practices were. Present the information you learned to your partner. Read the example.

I interviewed three people. The first one, my friend Nor, told me that until very recently, her company paid no attention to sustainability. But employees started to pressure them, so they put recycling bins in all the offices and asked everyone to cut down on their use of paper. Nor really cares about sustainability and thinks they are not doing enough, but at least it's a start. She and her co-workers are going to continue to pressure the company to do more.

Step 6 Talk!

PAIRS Sustainability at work makes good business sense. Employees want to work for companies that are environmentally responsible. Read some tips to help make your company or your personal life more sustainable. Discuss them using the questions below.

Make sure you use recycled packaging.

Allow employees to take home used office equipment and furniture.

Sell overstock items or less than perfect products, or donate them to a charity.

Decorate the office with plants to clean the air and remind workers of the environment.

Organize carpools or offer telecommuting.

Start a compost collection for food waste in the lunchroom.

Go paperless, print double sided, and reuse paper.

Offer a reward for employees to think of new ways to support sustainability.

- Which practices are you familiar with? Which practices are new to you?
- Which practices are most likely to be successful? Why?
- Which practices can have the most impact? Why?

Step 7 Going forward

A PAIRS In your online course, you reflected on how you could better support sustainability. Discuss. Listen to the examples.

B SHARE Present your ideas to the class.

VOCABULARY PRACTICE Go to page 82.

I can explain what business sustainability is. ☐

10

MODULE

Branding

Creating a Career Portfolio

DISCUSSION STRATEGIES

Go to page 68.

Step 1 Get started

A Refresh your memory! Watch the *What You'll Learn* video.

B Look at the photo. The job applicant presents her portfolio at a job interview. What do you think she included in her career portfolio?

C Check your understanding. Go to page 63.

Step 2 Tell your story

A THINK In your online course, you thought about a time you tried to create a résumé or another component of a career portfolio. What happened, and what did you learn? Listen to the example.

B PAIRS Discuss your story.

C SHARE Tell your story to the class.

Step 3 Activate your knowledge

A PAIRS Teri wants to apply for a job as a graphic designer. Read the job posting. Then read parts of Teri's career portfolio and explain the positive and negative aspects for each one. Take notes.

Graphic Designer—Global Financial Services

Graphic designers are responsible for interacting with the marketing team to design logos, brochures, marketing presentations, and website and social media content.

A successful candidate must have excellent design skills and be able to communicate design concepts to the marketing team. Experience with design software such as Adobe Photoshop and Adobe InDesign is essential. Understanding of the financial services industry is a plus. The candidate must be professional, creative, flexible, a team player, and able to meet deadlines with minimal supervision. [Mandarin recommended]

Career Summary: I have worked as a graphic designer for a food manufacturer for the past two years. I enjoy the challenge of working with the marketing department to create original designs that will communicate our brand to the public.

Skills	Design logos and create web content for advertising campaigns.
Career highlights	In my first year on the job, my logo design was selected out of 25 options. I am the lead designer on our current advertising campaign.

1

Positive: ______________________________

Negative: ______________________________

Biography: I grew up in a large family with my parents, grandparents, and four siblings. I was a good student. I studied Mandarin at school. In my free time, I enjoyed singing and dancing. I decided to become a graphic designer because it seemed like an interesting career.

2

Positive: ______________________________

Negative: ______________________________

Skills and Abilities:

Professional skills	Design logos, online and print advertising campaigns, and websites
Communication	Skilled at communicating design concepts. Speak Mandarin.
Time management	Always meet deadlines. Able to work independently.
Experience	Two years in graphic design
Computers	Proficient in design software
Education	BA in graphic design

3

Positive: ______________________________

Negative: ______________________________

B PAIRS Give Teri some suggestions on how she could improve her portfolio.

Career summary: ______________________________

Biography: ______________________________

Skills and abilities: ______________________________

C SHARE Present your suggestions to the class.

Step 4 Take away

GROUPS of 3–5 Match the example to the section in a career portfolio where you might find it.

	Example:
1. ___ contact page	a. a copy of a diploma
2. ___ career summary	b. social media account
3. ___ biography	c. education and training
4. ___ résumé	d. can type 60 words per minute
5. ___ skills and abilities	e. sketches or designs
6. ___ work samples	f. chess club trophy
7. ___ volunteer service	g. name of a university professor
8. ___ awards and honors	h. information about your family
9. ___ official documents	i. future goals
10. ___ references	j. participated in the Food for the Hungry campaign

Step 5 Project

PAIRS In your online course, you searched for a job you would like to have and prepared three components of your career portfolio: a career summary, a biography, and a list of skills and abilities. Present the information to your partner. Read the example.

The job posting I found was for a high school history teacher. I've recently graduated from university, but I've never taught before. I was a history major, and I took three education classes. In the career summary, I put information about my experience as a camp counselor. I included the ages of the campers because it shows that I have experience working with teenagers. I also talked about how I got interested in history and why I decided to become a teacher. I used as much language from the job posting as I could, like dedicated, passionate about teaching, responsible, trustworthy, *and* creative.

Step 6 Talk!

PAIRS A career portfolio is a great way to highlight your professional life. Look at the benefits. Then use the questions below to guide your conversation.

A career portfolio...

- provides a unique alternative to show your strengths
- tells your story in an interesting way
- allows you to stand out from the competition
- paints a more complete picture of you
- helps you to see your successes
- lets employers get a better idea of who you are
- gives you a chance to show your creativity

- Which benefit is the most important one for you?
- Which benefit is the least important one for you?
- Is a career portfolio always beneficial? In what instance might it be unnecessary?

Step 7 Going forward

A PAIRS In your online course, you reflected on how you could start to create a career portfolio. Discuss. Listen to the example.

B SHARE Present your ideas to the class.

VOCABULARY PRACTICE
Go to page 83.

I can explain how to create a career portfolio. ☐

11 MODULE

Job Search

The Information Interview

DISCUSSION STRATEGIES

Go to page 68.

Step 1 Get started

A Refresh your memory! Watch the *What You'll Learn* video.

B Look at the photo. Magda is conducting an information interview. What are some questions she might be asking?

C Check your understanding. Go to page 64.

Step 2 Tell your story

A THINK In your online course, you thought about a time you searched for a job. What happened, and what did you learn? Listen to the example.

B PAIRS Discuss your story.

C SHARE Tell your story to the class.

Step 3 Activate your knowledge

A PAIRS Read and listen to the excerpts from three informational interviews. What did each interviewer want to learn. Take notes.

INTERVIEW 1

Camila: So, I'm really curious...I'm sure that with your background and skills, you could have gotten a job just about anywhere. Why did you choose this particular company?

Interviewee: Because it was the only one that would take me? Seriously, though, that's a great question. I do my best work when I'm given a lot of freedom. And this company is known for hiring good people, and then getting out of their way to let them do their jobs. Having that kind of freedom—not having someone looking over my shoulder all the time— gives me the space I need to be creative.

INTERVIEW 2

Taner: Thank you for meeting with me today. Well, first of all, I was wondering if you could tell me some things that you dislike about your job?

Interviewee: Well...hmmm...that's rather straightforward of you, and it's kind of a strange question to start with. But anyway, nobody likes everything about their jobs, right? But for the most part, I'd say I'm pretty satisfied.

INTERVIEW 3

Paige: Thank you so much. That information was really useful. Do you have time for another question?

Interviewee: Sure, go ahead.

Paige: Well, I'm thinking about my next steps, and most of the jobs I've seen posted online require at least a year's experience. So, I was wondering what kind of entry-level job would give me the experience I need.

Interviewee: Hmm. Let me think. I suggest looking for a job as an administrative assistant or secretary at a law firm. Those jobs usually don't require experience or a legal background, but by working there you'll learn a lot about the law. Then you can put that experience on your résumé and apply for a position as a legal assistant.

B PAIRS Listen again. How successful were they in getting information. On a scale of 1-3, 1 is not very, 2 is somewhat, 3 very. Explain your answer by referring to the interviewee's response. Take notes in the chart. Then discuss your answers.

Interview	1 2 3	Explanation
1 Camila 	1 2 3	
2 Taner 	1 2 3	
3 Paige 	1 2 3	

C SHARE Present your answers and explanations to the class.

Step 4 Take away

A PAIRS Think about how to do an informational interview. Complete the steps.

thank-you potential candidate respectful carefully appropriately professional questions

1. Arrange the interview
   - identify ______________ interviewees
   - look up interviewees on ______________ websites
   - contact the best ______________
2. Prepare the interview
   - put together a list of ______________
   - find out how to dress ______________
3. Conduct the interview
   - be ______________ of interviewee's time
   - listen ______________ and take notes
   - follow-up with a ______________ email

B SHARE Compare your answers with another pair's.

Step 5 Project

PAIRS In your online course, you prepared for an informational interview by deciding on the purpose of the interview and making a list of questions for the interviewee. Share with your partner the purpose of the interview, the questions, and what you learned from the process. Read the example.

I've been thinking about changing careers, and I wanted to find out if electrical engineering was the right choice for me. The questions I prepared were: What do you like about being an electrical engineer? What do you wish you had known when you started your career? What are the opportunities in this field right now?

I learned a lot from having to really think about my purpose and then making up questions that would get me the information I wanted. I realize that although I'm interested in electrical engineering, I need to find out more about the field before I decide if it's the right career for me.

Step 6 Talk!

PAIRS Finding and getting a job can be challenging. Read these facts about job hunting. Then discuss them using the questions below.

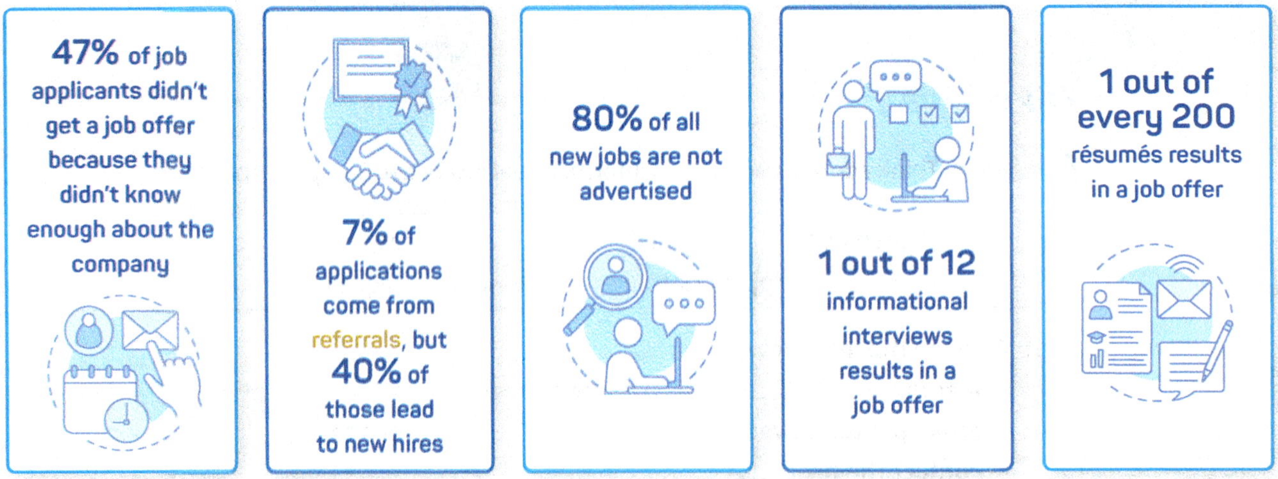

- What do you find most surprising about these facts?
- What conclusions can you draw about job-hunting, based on these facts?
- Will you change anything you do when you look for a job, based on these facts?

Step 7 Going forward

A **PAIRS** In your online course, you reflected on what you have learned about informational interviews and how you should prepare for one. Listen to the example.

B **SHARE** Present your ideas to the class.

VOCABULARY PRACTICE
Go to page 84.

I can explain how to have an informational interview. ☐

12

MODULE

Interviewing

The Interview

DISCUSSION STRATEGIES

Go to page 68.

Step 1 Get started

A Refresh your memory! Watch the *What You'll Learn* video.

B Look at the photo. Look at the woman being interviewed. How do you think she feels? How do you feel about interviewing? What can you do to prepare?

C Check your understanding. Go to page 65.

Step 2 Tell your story

A THINK In your online course, you thought about a time you interviewed for a job or other opportunity. What happened, and what did you learn? Listen to the example.

B PAIRS Discuss your story.

C SHARE Tell your story to the class.

Step 3 Activate your knowledge

A PAIRS Krystyna has a job interview. First, read the job posting and the information about Krystyna. Then read Krystyna's prepared answers to sample interview questions. Check what is missing from her answers.

A landscape gardening company seeking a team supervisor. In addition to having excellent landscaping skills, the ideal candidate will...

- have training in landscape design
- have strong leadership skills
- be able to work with all people with varying skill levels
- enjoy teamwork
- be physically fit

Krystyna Nowak

Experience
- Worked as a landscaper for the past five years, with three different companies

Education
- Completed several courses in landscape design
- High school diploma

Skills
- Landscape design and maintenance
- Able to lift 50 pounds

Interests
- Teaching children about gardening
- Running, biking, and softball
- Physical fitness

Personal traits
- A natural leader
- A team player

1. Tell me about yourself.

I'm a hard worker and really enjoy working with my hands. I like working outdoors, exercising, and working with kids.

_____ examples of her personal interests
_____ a description of her personality
_____ what makes her special
_____ key words from the job posting
_____ nothing is missing

2. Why do you want this job?

I have a passion for creating beautiful outdoor spaces, and I love sharing that passion with others. In my previous jobs, I took on a leadership role by training less skilled team members. With my skills, training, and experience, I know I will make an excellent team leader. I also want to continue developing my skills, and your company is well known for innovative design. I think this would be a great fit for both of us.

_____ her experience and/or education
_____ why this job makes sense for her
_____ key words from the job description
_____ something positive about the company
_____ nothing is missing

3. Tell me about a difficult situation you faced and how you handled it.

When I had my first job as a landscaper, I wasn't confident about my skills. Most of the landscapers had been working for many years. But I quickly realized that I knew as much as anyone else. And I could do as much heavy work as they could.

_____ the difficulty (be specific)
_____ how she handled it (be specific)
_____ the positive solution
_____ key words from the job description
_____ nothing is missing

4. What are your future goals?

First, I want to be an excellent team leader. Then I want to take courses in advanced landscape design and apply to your mentoring program. My goal is to become a landscape designer.

_____ contributions she will make to the job or company
_____ her long-term goals
_____ the match between her long-term goals and the opportunities available
_____ nothing is missing

B GROUPS Share your answers with the class.

Step 4 Take away

A PAIRS Review your notes from the online module and complete the most common interview questions with words from the box.

describe	good fit	shortcoming	difficult situations
characteristics	goals	leave	qualifications

1. Do you think you are a ______________________ for this position?
2. Why do you want to ______________________ your current job?
3. How would you ______________________ yourself?
4. What are your ______________________ for the future?
5. What are your ______________________ and why should you get this job?
6. How do you handle ______________________?
7. What personal ______________________ would help you excel here?
8. What is your greatest ______________________ or weakness?

B SHARE Check your answers with the class.

Step 5 Project

PAIRS In your online course, you researched a job that you wanted. You prepared to apply for it by answering the eight most common interview questions. Share the job, the key words in the job description, your answers to the questions, and what you learned from the process with your partner. Read the example.

The job I found was for a residence manager at a university. Some of the key words in the job description were reliable, level-headed, and good in a crisis. Here's my answer to "Why are you a good fit for the job?"
I worked as an Emergency Medical Technician. Many times I had to deal with crisis situations. I was able to remain level-headed, even when making important decisions. It was a stressful job, but I was the most reliable member of the team. I think my experience in crisis situations and my ability to handle stress makes me an excellent fit for this position.

Step 6 Talk!

PAIRS During a job interview, you could be asked almost anything. Here are some unusual interview questions. Read them, and then use the questions below to guide your conversation.

1. **What song best describes your work ethic?**
2. **Would you rather fight 1 horse-sized chicken or 100 chicken-sized horses?**
3. **Name four uses of a stapler without staple pins.**
4. **Desk, room, or car—which do you clean first?**
5. **If you could be a superhero, what would be your superpower?**
6. **If you were a brand, what would your motto be?**
7. **An apple costs 20 cents and an orange costs 40 cents. How much is a pear? Explain.**
8. **How strange are you? Rate yourself on a scale of 1 to 10.**
9. **What do you think of garden gnomes?**

- Do you have experience with any of these types of unusual interview questions? Explain.
- Discuss each question. What do you think the employer is trying to learn?
- Which questions could you answer well? Which would be the most difficult?

Step 7 Going forward

A PAIRS In your online course, you reflected on what you have learned about common interview questions. Listen to the example.

B SHARE Present your ideas to the class.

VOCABULARY PRACTICE Go to page 85.

I can explain how to prepare for a good job interview. ☐

CHECK YOUR UNDERSTANDING

Check your understanding 1

REFRESH YOUR MEMORY!
Review the Online Course material in your Resources.

Choose the best answers. More than one answer may be correct in some items.

1 **Conflict most often occurs when people ____.**
- **a** have serious disagreements
- **b** listen without interrupting
- **c** attempt to find a compromise

2 **In which scenario is someone using good listening techniques?**
- **a** Before Jann finishes explaining her concerns, Darden starts to write down his response.
- **b** Bill says to Jian, "You're saying that people don't respect your work. Is that right?"
- **c** Errol looks at his phone as Jim expresses his concerns, then asks Jim to get to the point.

3 **When people use "I" statements during the conflict-resolution process, they are ____.**
- **a** admitting that they caused the conflict
- **b** taking responsibility for their feelings
- **c** avoiding accusing others of causing the conflict

4 **Empathizing is important when working to resolve a conflict because it can ____.**
- **a** make the person who is empathizing feel important
- **b** help one person understand why another person is upset
- **c** show which party in a conflict is responsible for the problem

5 **Becca and Claire take turns driving each other to and from work every day. Claire always keeps Becca waiting, and they are often late for work. Becca keeps her feelings to herself until one morning when she is really angry and says, "We're always late because of you. I'm going to drive alone from now on." Claire is surprised and upset. To manage the conflict better, Becca could have said ____.**
- **a** "Either you stop keeping me waiting, or I'm going to drive to work by myself from now on."
- **b** "We can't continue to be late for work. Can we talk about how we can leave on time?"
- **c** "Riding together isn't working for me, and I'm going to drive to work by myself from now on."

6 **In a meeting to discuss a work conflict, Janice tells Simon that he often ignores her suggestions and does what he wants instead. Simon says, "I think you're saying that you don't feel like I value your ideas. Is that right?" Why does Simon clarify what Janice says?**
- **a** to explain why he does not agree with her
- **b** to help her learn to state things more clearly
- **c** to show that he understands her concern

7 **The co-managers of a popular restaurant disagree about the number of servers needed to provide the best service for their customers. They meet to come up with a list of ideas for resolving their conflict. This conflict-resolution strategy is called ____.**
- **a** compromising
- **b** active listening
- **c** brainstorming

8 **Greta and Li meet to discuss a conflict over sharing office space. They work out a compromise that gives both of them something they need. What should they say to each other before ending the meeting?**
- **a** "I didn't get what I wanted. I hope this works."
- **b** "I'm sorry if you're not happy with the outcome."
- **c** "Thank you for your willingness to resolve our conflict."

Check your understanding 2

REFRESH YOUR MEMORY!

Review the Online Course material in your Resources.

Choose the best answers. More than one answer may be correct in some items.

1 When someone gives you information that is confusing or unclear, you should ___.

a make your best guess about what the person means to say

b ignore the information, rather than doing something wrong

c ask the person to clarify the information to avoid mistakes

2 It is important to check facts and figures before sharing information because inaccurate information can ___.

a result in costly mistakes

b cause someone to lose their job

c prove that nobody is perfect

3 Which situation could put a customer relationship at risk?

a A salesperson suggests that a customer has poor taste in clothing.

b A customer waiting for help is told that someone is on the way.

c A manager loses his temper at a client for not returning his calls.

4 After making a serious communication mistake, a person should ___.

a explain that other people were involved in the error

b figure out what went wrong and learn from it

c take responsibility for the mistake and try to correct it

5 Sam accidentally sends his boss an early draft of an email. His boss spends a few minutes trying to make sense of it before going to Sam to ask for clarification. Sam is very embarrassed that his boss read an early draft that contained many errors. What can Sam learn from this experience?

a to reread email messages before hitting send

b to avoid sending emails to his boss

c to destroy drafts of written documents

6 During a large team meeting, a manager blames an employee for losing an important customer by forgetting to pass along a message. What should the manager have done instead?

a She should have mentioned the error and asked the team to find out who was at fault.

b She should have spoken with the employee privately to avoid embarrassing him.

c She should have taken the blame herself to avoid embarrassing the employee.

7 Marcos writes a letter to everyone who donated to his organization, thanking them for their generosity. After sending the letters out by email, he discovers that he left "Dear ___," as the greeting. He had forgotten to replace the blank spaces with each person's name. What should Marcos do?

a Leave things as they are, knowing people will understand.

b Email an apology without fixing the letter or sending it out again.

c Resend the letter with the names filled in, and include an apology.

8 A construction manager orders windows for a house she is building. When the windows arrive, she realizes that they are not exactly what the customer had asked for, but are exactly what the manager ordered. What is the first thing the manager should do?

a Tell the customer what happened and accept responsibility for fixing the mistake.

b Take the blame and apologize for the mistake but install the wrong windows, anyway.

c Install the windows without mentioning the error and hope the customer likes them.

Check your understanding 3

REFRESH YOUR MEMORY!
Review the Online Course material in your Resources.

Choose the best answers. More than one answer may be correct in some items.

1 Why is it important to monitor progress toward your goals?

a so that your friends and family can see that your plan is working
b so that you know if and when you have to make adjustments
c so that you can be sure you and your plan are on track to succeed

2 Which list includes the most important steps toward reaching a goal?

a Check progress often, measure progress appropriately, share progress with others.
b Get input from others, set check-in reminders, revise goals often.
c Discuss goals with professionals, use social media to report progress, measure success.

3 Which is an effective monitoring technique?

a Set times to evaluate progress toward your goal.
b Discuss your goal with an expert on the subject.
c Commit to a timeline for reaching your goal.

4 What is the main reason for sharing your goals and your progress with other people?

a Sharing gives others a chance to make suggestions about your goals.
b Other people can help you continue to monitor your progress toward your goals.
c Making others aware of your goals pushes you to keep working toward them.

5 Strategies to help you meet your goals should include ____.

a talking with friends and family about your goals
b determining numerous ways to measure progress
d checking-in often to think about how you are doing

6 Aria is planning a trip during which she will be hiking approximately ten miles every day. Her goal is to be able to do a 10-mile walk before the trip. To prepare, she has been walking daily for two months. To be sure she is making progress toward her goal, Aria should monitor ____.

a the time it takes her to walk a mile
b the number of miles she walks each day
c the number of steps she takes per mile

7 Michael wants to change jobs within six months. He decides to apply to one job every week, but he does not put his plan in writing. As a result, he stops sending applications after the first month. What can he do to ensure that he gets back to making progress toward his goal?

a Tell his family or friends about his goal and share his progress with them.
b Write down details of his plan and check regularly to be sure they are getting done.
c Put his search on hold until he is ready to commit to a more serious effort.

8 The sales manager of an online T-shirt company has just launched a new website. Her goal is to increase T-shirt sales from 400 to 1,000 shirts per week within six months. To monitor progress toward her goal, the sales manager should ____.

a check in weekly to see how many people have clicked on the site and how many have subscribed to the company's promotional emails
b keep track of the number of T-shirts sold every week to see if total sales are increasing by about 100 shirts each month
c keep a written record of the company's weekly sales income to make sure it is increasing steadily throughout the six-month period

Check your understanding 4

REFRESH YOUR MEMORY! Review the Online Course material in your Resources.

Choose the best answers. More than one answer may be correct in some items.

1 Why is it important to establish clear goals for the members of a team?

a Goals allow team members to do their work without any supervision.

b Clear goals help the team focus on the most important aspects of their jobs.

c Goals help team members understand what they have to do and why they are doing it.

2 Building trust with a team involves ____.

a treating all team members fairly and equally

b monitoring workers closely throughout the day

c keeping an open mind and communicating clearly

3 One way to improve team performance and help a team reach its goals is to define workers' roles. This means managers should ____.

a assign each team member specific responsibilities

b allow team members to choose tasks they enjoy most

c hire additional workers to do tasks that others don't like

4 In which description does a team member show signs of reduced engagement?

a Jared believes he has outgrown his job, and he asks his boss about a promotion.

b Ruth seems distracted at work, and she has taken a lot of sick and vacation time.

c Dinah and her team complete a big project, and some of them request time off.

5 An easy-to-use information sharing system helps team members succeed because ____.

a everybody has equal access to the materials they need to do their work

b certain managers can check the work of all members of their team

c updated schedules and other details can all be found in one place

6 Every morning, the editor of a small newspaper holds a brief meeting. She tells each reporter what stories to cover that day. Then she invites them to ask questions. She responds clearly and wishes them luck. How does this approach help the team?

a By focusing on clear goals, team members know exactly how to proceed with their work.

b Asking questions and getting clear answers eliminates confusion about meeting their goals.

c Because the editor thinks through the details, team members are not required to work hard.

7 In a weekly meeting, Damien reports that his work is going well but then causes the team to miss an important deadline. How will this affect the other team members?

a They will no longer feel enthusiastic about their jobs.

b They will lose trust in Damien and stop believing what he says.

c They will refuse to work toward their goals in the future.

8 Youssef is the manager of a new movie theater. He hires twelve employees and shows all of them how to sell tickets, run the concession stand, collect tickets, and seat customers. Then he gives them a schedule so they know when to report for work. When the first team arrives at work, everybody goes to the concession stand. What did Youssef forget to do?

a Assign a clear role to each member of the team.

b Clarify the responsibilities of each type of job.

c Build trust among the members of each team.

9 Li works in a preschool. At first, she enjoys the job and the children. Then she notices that her co-workers exclude her from conversations and plan class activities without discussing them with her. She no longer enjoys her job, and she starts calling in sick frequently. This means the other team members have to cover Li's responsibilities. How should the team's supervisor address this situation?

a She should take disciplinary action against the other team members for excluding Li.

b She should tell Li to take time off and return when she is ready to be a team player.

c She should ask Li what is bothering her, then help her come up with a solution.

10 When Jaz starts working for an advertising agency, she and her team frequently get together to share ideas. Then the agency decides that everyone will work remotely, and they close the office. Without frequent team feedback, Jaz does not know if her ideas are realistic. She misses the support of her teammates and her team is not as successful as it was previously. What can be done to address this situation?

a Team members can schedule frequent videoconferences to ask questions and react to their co-workers' ideas.

b The team's supervisor can work individually with team members to review work and provide one-to-one feedback.

c The agency can provide software that will enable employees to share their work and comment on the work of others.

Check your understanding 5

REFRESH YOUR MEMORY!
Review the Online Course material in your Resources.

Choose the best answers. More than one answer may be correct in some items.

1 **What are important steps in the critical-thinking process?**
- **a** Determine the writer's reason for providing the information.
- **b** Consider whether the information is factual and verifiable.
- **c** Determine whether the writer has the same opinion as you do.

2 **Why is it important to know something about the source of the information you read?**
- **a** to understand how the writer feels about the subject
- **b** to make sure the writer is a specialist in the field
- **c** to determine whether the information is trustworthy

3 **In which case is the information in a scientific article likely to be unreliable?**
- **a** It appears on a website ending in .edu.
- **b** The writer is selling a related product.
- **c** The data are from a peer-reviewed study.

4 **To determine whether information is reliable or unreliable, a reader should ask:**
- **a** Where does the information come from?
- **b** When was the information created?
- **c** What is the author's personal opinion?

5 **When Tuyet was looking for a new car, she relied on car manufacturers' websites for information about various models. Every screen included beautiful photographs and positive descriptions. Every model seemed perfect. How could Tuyet have gotten information that was reliable and unbiased, instead?**
- **a** She could have included information about cars she was not interested in buying.
- **b** She could have read articles written by independent researchers and reviewers.
- **c** She could have spoken directly to people who sell the cars she's considering.

6 **Listening to a favorite podcast, Rafael hears about an online course that helps people overcome their fear of public speaking. He thinks this could help him realize his dream of teaching Spanish. What can he do to find out whether the course really works?**
- **a** Contact someone who works for the company that is promoting the online course.
- **b** Research public-speaking courses on a website with a domain name ending in .edu.
- **c** Read the student testimonials that the company has selected for its website.

7 **Elyse is a personal trainer who specializes in coaching marathon runners. She often conducts online research to stay current with the latest training practices. In one article, a company claims, "Our revolutionary workout method is guaranteed to improve race times by ten minutes or more." Why should Elyse question the accuracy of this claim?**
- **a** It includes language that may be deceptive.
- **b** The company is trying to sell a product.
- **c** Companies cannot guarantee their products.

8 **The IT manager for a small company wants to buy laptops for the company's employees. He reads online reviews to find out which stores provide the best products and the best service. On one company's website, several reviews include this information: "This review was provided in response to a promotion." What should the IT manager consider when evaluating these reviews?**
- **a** They are honest, accurate reviews written by actual customers.
- **b** They may not reflect customers' actual experiences and opinions.
- **c** The writers of these reviews may have included misleading information.

Check your understanding 6

REFRESH YOUR MEMORY!
Review the Online Course material in your Resources.

Choose the best answers. More than one answer may be correct in some items.

1 **Good leadership involves ____.**
- **a** getting people to work well together
- **b** letting others make most of the decisions
- **c** monitoring workers at all times

2 **The most successful leaders ____.**
- **a** ask for and consider other people's ideas
- **b** take charge and organize work for the team
- **c** observe rather than take part in tasks

3 **Ways an effective leader coordinates tasks for the team include ____.**
- **a** keeping people who don't get along from working together
- **b** matching tasks with team members' interests and strengths
- **c** sharing decision-making responsibilities with team members

4 **How does a leader make sure that everyone shares responsibility?**
- **a** by demonstrating how to do each of the tasks
- **b** by working with every team to get the job done
- **c** by coordinating tasks to match people's skills

5 **Rosa has worked at a daycare center for many years. When she is promoted to supervisor, her responsibilities include planning each day's activities and assigning her co-workers to various jobs. At their weekly meetings, Rosa asks the team for creative ideas about activities for the children, but she never follows through on them. Her co-workers are often confused about what they are expected to do. What leadership skills does Rosa need to improve?**
- **a** She needs to organize the work better.
- **b** She needs to listen to other peoples' ideas.
- **c** She needs to get everyone to cooperate.

6 **At the beginning of the summer, counselors at Kidsports Camp arrive early to get the sports equipment out of the storage barn and set it up for the campers. This requires a lot of coordination among counselors, many of whom are new to the camp. How can team leaders ensure that the job goes smoothly?**
- **a** Encourage cooperation by matching experienced counselors with first-time counselors and having them work together.
- **b** Decide which team of counselors will do which jobs, making sure that all of the jobs are assigned.
- **c** Let each counselor decide for themselves what needs to be done and who will be responsible for each of the tasks.

7 **The owner of a small bookstore has ordered new shelving to display their books. He asks the employees if anyone is able to stay after work to pack boxes of books, but nobody volunteers. What can he do to encourage the employees to help?**
- **a** He can suggest they work in teams to get the work done faster.
- **b** He can express his disappointment that nobody cares enough to help.
- **c** He can offer to buy pizza and drinks for anyone who stays to help.

8 **Sophia is an assistant manager on a family farm. Every morning, she meets with workers to talk about the day's goals. One morning after a very rainy weekend, she notices that the field she planned to work in is flooded, and she is not sure what the team can work on instead. Which approach shows good leadership skills?**
- **a** Stick with the original plan, even if she knows it will damage the crops.
- **b** Ask workers if they have any ideas, and listen to what they have to say.
- **c** Let workers do whatever they want to do until the field dries up.

Check your understanding 7

REFRESH YOUR MEMORY!

Review the Online Course material in your Resources.

Choose the best answers. More than one answer may be correct in some items.

1 **One reason people procrastinate is because they have to do something that is ____.**

a urgent or important

b complicated or confusing

c easy and enjoyable

2 **Procrastination usually involves ____.**

a putting something off rather than getting it done in a timely way

b creating distractions that keep us from doing things we may not want to do

c getting things done early to allow time for things we would rather be doing

3 **What are common reasons for procrastinating?**

a We do not understand a task and worry that we will make mistakes.

b The task involves things we do not enjoy, so we avoid getting started.

c We know exactly what needs to be done and how to do it.

4 **What happens when procrastinating keeps people from making progress and meeting deadlines?**

a They feel guilty and stressed, which can make it hard to focus on the work.

b They experience a "snowball effect," which means other things do not get done, either.

c They are better able to think through the tasks and create a plan to complete the work.

5 **When a task is so big you do not know where to begin, it is a good idea to ____.**

a break it down into smaller tasks that are easier to accomplish

b cut out difficult aspects of the task and do only what is easy

c delay until the deadline is near so the only choice is to get started

6 **Richard is supposed to present the results of his team's research project in a PowerPoint presentation. He is overwhelmed by the amount of information he needs to present, and he has been avoiding the work. What would make it easier for him to get the work done?**

a breaking the job into small tasks instead of looking at it as one overwhelming task

b doing the easiest pieces first and saving the largest, most difficult ones until the end

c doing one of the difficult tasks first so the project doesn't seem so overwhelming

7 **Part of Georgette's new job at a garden center is ordering seeds for sale in the spring. Because she is worried about making poor choices, she distracts herself with other tasks until the ordering deadline is just days away. What should Georgette do to complete the order before it is too late?**

a She should email other garden centers to see what their customers buy.

b She should ask her boss for guidance about what the customers like.

c She should plan to reward herself if she meets the deadline

8 **Carlo's least favorite thing about teaching high school English is having to spend evenings and weekends correcting papers. He sometimes puts the work off, and then he has to work even harder to get everything done. What can he do to help make the task more appealing?**

a Work late every night so he can finish the papers in fewer days.

b Take breaks between papers to have a snack or talk with a friend.

c Create a schedule for completing all papers and be sure to stick to it.

Check your understanding 8

REFRESH YOUR MEMORY! Review the Online Course material in your Resources.

Choose the best answers. More than one answer may be correct in some items.

1 Emotional stress can come from ___.

- **a** developing bad sleeping habits
- **b** having to do too many things at one time
- **c** pressure to be successful in your job

2 Practical stressors are brought about by ___.

- **a** important changes in our lives
- **b** events that are outside our control
- **c** everyday situations and events

3 Change-related stressors include ___.

- **a** starting a new job
- **b** buying a house
- **c** getting sick

4 Stress sometimes causes people to develop unhealthy habits and avoid important commitments. These signs are considered ___.

- **a** physical signs of stress
- **b** emotional signs of stress
- **c** behavioral signs of stress

5 Jacob's mother is ill, and he has been leaving work early twice a week to help take care of her. His boss keeps asking him when he will be able to complete a sales report. In response to this situation, Jacob is likely to experience ___.

- **a** emotional stress
- **b** practical stress
- **c** change-related stress

6 A worker is promoted to a demanding management position that requires frequent out-of-state travel. When he is away for work, he misses his family, and he is unable to keep up with things at home. What symptoms might he experience as a result of stress from his new position?

- **a** behavior changes, such as avoiding work and family
- **b** emotional symptoms, like frustration and anxiety
- **c** physical symptoms, such as high blood pressure

7 A husband and wife return to their jobs weeks after their baby is born. They soon find that it is difficult to concentrate on their work with the new responsibilities of parenting. They have not been making time for exercise, healthy meals, or relaxation. What kind of stress are they experiencing?

- **a** physical
- **b** emotional
- **c** behavioral

8 A couple buys an old house that needs a lot of work. They are soon spending all of their nights and weekends and much of their savings on house repairs. They miss going hiking and getting together with friends. What would help them reduce the stress of constant work?

- **a** Write down every evening how much they accomplished that day.
- **b** Set aside time each week to go for a hike, take a short trip, or visit friends.
- **c** Work harder and longer so that they can finish the house sooner.

9 Tran's office at work is piled high with books, files, and personal belongings. He often misses work deadlines and his boss has warned that he will be replaced if things do not improve. Tran starts getting headaches and stomachaches before work each day. What steps can he take to manage his stress?

- **a** look for another job
- **b** clean and rearrange his office
- **c** create a time management plan

Check your understanding 9

REFRESH YOUR MEMORY! Review the Online Course material in your Resources.

Choose the best answers. More than one answer may be correct in some items.

1 **In the business world, "sustainability" means ____.**
- **a** replacing workers with automation
- **b** hiring workers from the local community
- **c** taking care of people, profits, and the environment

2 **The CEO of a manufacturing company invests in solar panels and batteries to replace electricity generated by using fossil fuels. This decision shows a commitment to ____.**
- **a** the health of the planet
- **b** the safety of employees
- **c** a future increase in profits

3 **Which business practice promotes sustainability of the planet?**
- **a** making all its products recyclable
- **b** sharing a percentage of company profits with employees
- **c** offering employees affordable apartments close to their work

4 **A successful boutique buys wedding dresses and other formal clothing from the manufacturer. Then the boutique rents the clothes to people for special occasions. When the rental period ends, customers return the clothing to the store, where it is cleaned, repaired if necessary, and offered for rent again. Does this practice contribute to profits, the planet, or both?**
- **a** profits only
- **b** the planet only
- **c** both profits and the planet

5 **The owners of a farm want to provide fresh produce twelve months of the year, but the winters are too cold to grow the produce outdoors. Instead, they need to grow it in large greenhouses that require a great deal of energy to heat. What kind of business sustainability practices can the farm's owners use?**
- **a** They can heat the greenhouses with solar power.
- **b** They can raise prices to pay the higher cost of electricity in winter.
- **c** They can hire fewer employees to save money in order to pay heating costs.

6 **A group of doctors opens a community health center within walking distance of 75% of the town's population. Low-income residents receive free medical and dental care. In what way does the center support sustainable practices?**
- **a** The doctors make more money than they would in a private office or hospital.
- **b** Its location allows people to walk or bicycle to visits rather than drive cars.
- **c** It shows that the doctors care about the health and well-being of all citizens.

7 **A chip-manufacturing company is opening a new plant just outside of a large city. The company will bring hundreds of new jobs to the area. What should the hiring managers do to support business sustainability as it relates to its workforce?**
- **a** Hire workers that represent the racial, economic, and educational diversity of the city.
- **b** Offer mostly part-time jobs with low salaries to give jobs to more people and increase profits.
- **c** Offer transportation, a healthy work environment, and fair wages to workers.

8 **Before offering space to renters, the owners of a new office building hire a sustainable-energy expert to make sure the building is efficient in its use of electricity and water. The results are very good. How can this information affect the building owners' profits?**
- **a** More people will rent offices when they learn that their electric and water bills will be low.
- **b** The owners will have a good reputation because of their commitment to the environment.
- **c** It will not affect profits because renters are interested in low rents more than sustainable energy.

Check your understanding 10

REFRESH YOUR MEMORY!
Review the Online Course material in your Resources.

Choose the best answers. More than one answer may be correct for some items.

1 What does a career portfolio include? Match the portfolio component on the left with a description on the right.

a Career summary	**i** career overview and future career plan
b Biography	**ii** skills and their relevance to the job
c Résumé	**iii** interests and unique personal traits
d Skills and abilities	**iv** plaques, trophies, and ribbons
e Work samples	**v** education and employment history
f Awards and honors	**vi** essays, reports, projects

2 How does your career portfolio help potential employers?

- **a** It shows them your skills, interests, and qualifications for a job.
- **b** It provides information about your private life.
- **c** It shows your individual personality.

3 What type of information should be included on the contact page?

- **a** LinkedIn URL profile
- **b** links to all social media accounts
- **c** email address and cell phone number

4 What should be included in a career summary page?

- **a** why you chose this career
- **b** what your future career expectations are
- **c** what interests you have besides your career

5 What should be included on a service page?

- **a** volunteer work experience
- **b** military service
- **c** your résumé

6 Which component of a career portfolio should include school transcripts, degrees, licenses, and certifications?

- **a** the volunteer service page
- **b** the awards page
- **c** the important documents page

7 Stella is an experienced landscape architect who specializes in parks and other public spaces. She is especially proud of the award-winning gardens she designed for a nearby state park, and she wants to feature them in her portfolio. How should Stella present this information?

- **a** Include a description of the gardens on the skills and abilities page and information about the awards on the awards and honors page.
- **b** Include photographs of the gardens in the work samples section and information about the awards on the awards and honors page.
- **c** Include photographs of the gardens in the work samples section and photographs of the awards in the important documents section.

8 When Jamal was working in his first job as a doctor, patients frequently posted compliments about him on his employer's website. They appreciated his calm approach in times of crisis, and they came to trust his judgment and his advice. Now, Jamal is moving across the country and looking for a new job. He wants to be sure potential employers know how his patients feel about him. How can he include this information in his career portfolio?

- **a** He can include the compliments on his biography page.
- **b** He can put the comments in with his important documents.
- **c** He can include copies of the comments in his references section.

9 Ying has won many awards and special honors as a lawyer and an athlete. Soon she will be moving to another city and looking for a new job. What awards and honors would be appropriate to include in her professional career portfolio?

- **a** professional awards and honors, only
- **b** all professional and personal awards and honors
- **c** work- and school-related honors, but not personal awards

10 Shobana is a software specialist who is seeking her first job as a video game designer. She has decided to provide her qualifications and some examples of her schoolwork in a softcopy portfolio. How should her portfolio be presented?

- **a** by sections in a three-ring binder
- **b** as a link to a website or presentation
- **c** in both a three-ring binder and in an online presentation

Check your understanding 11

REFRESH YOUR MEMORY!

Review the Online Course material in your Resources.

Choose the best answers. More than one answer may be correct in some items.

1 When should you schedule an informational interview?

a after submitting a cover letter and résumé in response to a job opening
b when thinking about changing jobs or careers
c after being offered a job, but before accepting it

2 After you have identified three people you might want to interview, what would help you decide which one to contact?

a Research the company where each of them works.
b Send each of them an email with a general question to see how they respond.
c Learn what you can about each of them from a professional networking site.

3 When preparing for an informational interview with someone who works where you want to work, you should ____.

a read about the company and prepare specific questions about the work
b familiarize yourself with technologies and terminology in the field
c research the kinds of jobs other people at the company do

4 What are important things to include when asking someone for an informational interview?

a when and where to conduct the interview
b what the interviewee likes about the job
c how long you expect the interview to take

5 Aman, a computer programmer, is considering changing careers. He talks with an energy-company representative at a job fair, who offers to meet Aman for an informational interview. Which questions will help him learn about careers in the field?

a What kinds of opportunities are available for a person with my background?
b What trends in the solar energy field are likely to provide future work?
c Why did you choose to pursue work with this particular company?

6 Before Sadia decides whether to go to graduate school for a degree in urban planning, she wants to learn more about the background, strengths, and skills required for a career in that field. She sets up an informational interview with the director of her city's planning department and starts to prepare a list of questions. What should she ask?

a What personality traits would help an urban planner be successful?
b Is there a lot of competition for jobs in this field?
c What kinds of skills and training are needed for a planning career?

7 Evan recently earned a license to drive delivery trucks, and he is gathering information about companies that hire drivers. He schedules an informational interview with the hiring manager of a local company. What questions would help Evan learn about working for this company?

a What other companies are currently hiring new drivers?
b How would you describe the culture of the company?
c What kind of entry-level job is a good place to start?

8 Amala is preparing for an informational interview at a nearby college to see if she is a good fit for a job as a dietician. What is an appropriate way for her to ask about the potential for advancement?

a Are there opportunities for growth for a dietician at the college?
b If I started working today, when could I expect to get promoted?
c What would be the highest salary for a person with my background and skills?

Check your understanding 12

REFRESH YOUR MEMORY! Review the Online Course material in your Resources.

Choose the best answers. More than one answer may be correct in some items.

1 **Why is it a good idea to prepare for the most common types of interview questions?**

- **a** Knowing how to answer common questions will make you more confident during the interview.
- **b** Preparing helps you to develop answers to some of the questions you will be asked.
- **c** Being well prepared shows the interviewer that you have a lot of interviewing experience.

2 **When an interviewer asks, "How did you like your previous job?," she wants to know ____.**

- **a** what your strengths and weaknesses are
- **b** why you are looking for a new job
- **c** what makes you qualified for the job

3 **When asked to describe yourself in an interview, how should you respond?**

- **a** Talk about your strengths and weaknesses as they relate to past jobs.
- **b** Describe positive personality traits and how you spend your free time.
- **c** Provide a brief history of your childhood, education, and work experience.

4 **An interviewer asks why you think you would be a good fit for the job. What do they want to know?**

- **a** what you already know about the company
- **b** why you applied for the position
- **c** what experiences have prepared you for the work

5 **If an interviewer asks you why you should be hired for the position, you should ____.**

- **a** describe the qualifications you have that best relate to the job
- **b** explain what might set you apart from other candidates
- **c** promise to work hard and stay with the company for a long time

6 **Johan has been an assistant librarian for three years. The head librarian announces her retirement, and Johan applies for the job. In his interview, he is asked, "What makes you a good candidate for a management job?" What kind of information is the interviewer asking for?**

- **a** what made Johan decide to become a librarian
- **b** what kinds of managerial experience Johan has had
- **c** what skills the retiring head has

7 **In an interview for a position with a publishing company, Ziporah is asked what her weaknesses are. She responds, "I sometimes hurry to finish my work, and my bosses have told me I would make fewer mistakes if I slowed down. They're probably right." What would have been a better response?**

- **a** "Because I don't like to miss deadlines, I sometimes rush through my work to finish in time. I don't like to make mistakes, so I'm learning to slow down and check my work."
- **b** "I've been told that I work too fast. But I think that's actually a good thing, because I never miss deadlines, and that is important in this kind of work."
- **c** "When I hurry through my work, I make some mistakes. I know that someone will catch them later, so this isn't really a problem."

8 **Kathryn has worked at the same company for six years, and it is clear that her boss is never going to give her new responsibilities. She decides it is time to find a new job that might offer her more challenging work. In a job interview, she is asked why she is leaving her job after so long. How can she explain her decision to move on?**

- **a** She should admit that she has gotten bored after doing the same thing for so long.
- **b** She should explain that her current boss has not given her any opportunities to grow.
- **c** She should say something nice about her company and tell the interviewer that she is ready for a new challenge.

9 **In an interview for a job at a car dealership, Ryan was asked to describe a time when he had to perform under pressure and how he handled it. What should Ryan remember to include in his response?**

- **a** A specific example of a stressful situation and how he got through it with positive results.
- **b** What valuable lesson he learned from having to work through a challenging situation.
- **c** How he has learned to handle work pressure and challenging situations in general.

10 **Anika has always wanted to teach history at the college level. In an interview for a position as an assistant professor at a state university she is asked about her future goals. Which response will prove that she would be a good candidate for the position?**

- **a** "I have been preparing since high school to teach at a college or a university, and I would like to be a full professor someday."
- **b** "I know that we all have to start somewhere, so for now, I'm just focusing on getting my first job doing something I love."
- **c** "I expect to move quickly from assistant professor to associate professor to full professor as others in this department have done."

DISCUSSION STRATEGIES

Discussion strategies

When you are in class or at work, you may need to take part in discussions. To successfully participate, you can use a number of different kinds of strategies. They include strategies that help you . . .

1 Work with others
2 Clarify what you hear or clarify what you say
3 Get and stay involved in the discussion
4 Organize your ideas

During each discussion in class, choose one kind of strategy you want to improve or one you think will be useful. Pick a phrase and try to use it during the in-class activities. Remember to always say the phrase in a polite way.

You can listen to the phrases and examples ▶.

1 Working with others

Some strategies can make it easier to work with other people who are part of the discussion. If you can, try starting the discussion or helping to keep the discussion moving in the right direction. These strategies can help.

Management strategies	Sample phrases
a Starting the discussion	▶ Are we ready to start? ▶ Let's begin. ▶ Who has an idea about this?
b Asking others to participate	▶ Who wants to answer? ▶ Does anyone have anything to add? ▶ Are there any other ideas?
c Helping specific people to get involved	▶ John, what do you think? ▶ Do you have anything to add, Kim? ▶ Carmen, what do you think of Jennifer's idea?
d Jumping in with talkative people	▶ That's a good idea, but now let's hear from other people. ▶ Let's hear what everyone else has to say. ▶ Pablo, you make a good point. Why don't we see what some others think?
e Staying on the topic	▶ That's interesting, but, sorry, I don't see how that fits our discussion. ▶ That's great, but we need to stay on topic. ▶ Hmm . . . I don't think that's really related to our topic.
f Keeping the discussion moving	▶ OK. Let's move to the next question. ▶ That's a great idea! We can talk about that if we have time at the end. ▶ Sorry, but we're going to run out of time if we don't get to the next point.
g Telling someone you can't hear them*	▶ I'm sorry. I didn't hear what you said. ▶ Can you speak a little louder, please? ▶ Sorry! What was that?
h Telling someone they speak too fast*	▶ I'm sorry. Can you say that a little slower? ▶ Can you speak more slowly, please? ▶ Sorry! I didn't catch that.

*You can also use clarification strategies to make sure you understood someone who is quiet or talks too quickly.

Discussion strategies

2 Clarifying

Sometimes, it is hard for you to understand what someone is saying or for others to understand you. Clarifying is a natural part of discussions. Even native speakers use these strategies because not everyone understands everything all the time!

Clarification strategies	Sample phrases	Examples
a Clarifying (when you didn't understand someone else)	Sorry, but . . . I'm not sure what you mean by . . . I didn't follow . . . I don't get it. Are you saying . . .?	Sorry, but I don't understand. I'm not sure what you mean by SMART goals. I didn't follow what you said. Could you go over that again? Sorry! I don't get it. Are you saying that we might miss the deadline?
b Restating (when someone doesn't understand you)	In other words . . . I mean . . .	**A:** Make your goal and your progress public. It's important to monitor your progress toward a goal. **B:** Sorry, but I don't understand. **A:** In other words, don't keep your goal and progress private. Telling others about them makes you more likely to succeed. **A:** It's important to monitor your progress toward a goal. **B:** I'm not sure what you mean by monitoring. **A:** By monitoring, I mean taking the time to notice how well you're doing something to help you achieve your goals.
c Checking (when you want to make sure someone understands you)	Just checking–do you know what I mean? Is that clear? Does anyone have any questions? Does what I've just said make sense?	
d Paraphrasing (what the speaker says)	Are you saying that . . . Do you mean that . . .	**A:** Miscommunication can lead to a lot of mistakes. **B:** Are you saying that we should try to avoid saying the wrong thing to customers? **A:** Saying the wrong thing to a customer can affect profits. **B:** Do you mean that we could lose money if we don't say the right thing?
e Paraphrasing (what someone else says)	Akemi said that . . . What . . . means is . . .	Akemi said that we should not try to hide our mistakes. We should admit them. What Alana means is that apologizing is better than making excuses.

Discussion strategies

3 Getting involved

It can be challenging to participate in discussions. Sometimes, you have to involve yourself without being asked, keep your turn (if others try to interrupt you), interrupt (when others are talking), and get your turn back (after being interrupted).

Participation strategies	Sample phrases	Examples
a Getting involved	Can I ask a question, please? Sorry to interrupt! But I have something I'd like to say. Sorry! Do you mind if I jump in here?	
b Keeping your turn	Excuse me. If you don't mind, I'd just like to finish what I was saying. Sorry, but could you please wait? I'm almost finished. Sorry, but could I just finish this one thought?	
c Interrupting	Excuse me . . . Sorry to interrupt . . . Sorry to cut in . . .	Excuse me, but I'd like to add something. Sorry to interrupt, but I have a question. Sorry to cut in, but I need to ask a question.
d Getting your turn back	As I was saying . . . Going back to what I was saying . . . In any case . . .	As I was saying, mistakes can actually make us better. Going back to what I was saying, there are four steps to take after we've made a mistake. In any case, the four steps to take remain the same.
e Commenting (on what someone has said)	That's a good point. I see what you mean. I have to agree with you.	
f Adding (to what someone has said)	I agree with you . . . and also . . . Another thing to consider is . . . I have something to add to that . . .	I agree with you about profits, Ben, and also, we need to keep customers happy. Yes, and another thing to consider is keeping customers happy. I have something to add to that. A lot of mistakes can't be fixed, so when you have the opportunity to fix one, be glad.

Discussion strategies

4 Organizing

Lastly, organization techniques can help communication and make discussion easier to follow.

Organization techniques	Sample words and phrases	Examples
a Chronological	First . . . second . . . third . . . Next . . . then . . . later	▶ First, identify what you both want. Second, brainstorm solutions. Third, make a plan. ▶ Next, we will talk about setting a schedule. Then we'll talk about including deadlines. Later, we'll discuss how we need to be open to changes.
b Cause and effect	If . . . , then . . . When . . . , then . . .	▶ If you try active listening, then you're more likely to resolve conflict. ▶ When you practice, then you learn to resolve conflicts.
c Categorical	There are five ways . . . The main thing . . .	▶ There are five ways to resolve conflict. ▶ The main thing to do is to communicate respectfully.
d Problem and solution	The main problem is . . . One big issue is . . . The best solution is . . . We could . . .	▶ The main problem is that we don't take responsibility for our own behavior and mistakes. ▶ One big issue is we don't use enough "I" messages. ▶ The best solution is to work together to avoid conflict. ▶ We could implement the five ways to avoid conflict.
e Adding an idea	Also, . . . In the same way, . . .	▶ Brainstorming is useful because it leads to a lot of ideas. Also, there are no right or wrong answers. ▶ You should set a schedule to work toward your solution. In the same way, you should include important details and deadlines.
f Contrast	Although . . . However, . . .	▶ Although thanking everyone who helped you work through the problem is important, thanking yourself is important, too! ▶ Active listening is challenging. However, it's worth the effort so we can avoid conflicts in the workplace.

VOCABULARY PRACTICE

Vocabulary practice 1

Exercise (A)

Complete the puzzle.

Across

1 a feeling of being a little angry
3 nervous, worried and not able to relax
8 to refuse to accept something
11 a claim that someone has done something wrong or illegal
12 to end a problem or challenge

Down

2 to reach agreement where each person or group gives up something to end an argument
4 to stop showing your feelings because you are upset
5 a feeling of anger and annoyance because you are unable to do something
6 to come up with a lot of ideas for a future activity
7 very anxious and quick to protect oneself from criticism
9 based on facts and not your personal beliefs or feelings
10 an act of stating that you are sorry for your actions or words that you think are wrong

Exercise (B)

Use the correct words from the puzzle to complete a student's notes.

HOW TO MANAGE CONFLICT

- When faced with a conflict, it is hard to [1] ______________ the urge to hide from it. Sometimes it's better to work through your [2] ______________ and accept the situation as it is.
- Before you can [3] ______________ a conflict, you should try to find out what caused it.
- Try not to be [4] ______________ if the other person is criticizing you. Shift your attention to the other person and try to understand their side.
- Try to be [5] ______________. Focus on the facts and not your emotions. If you only consider your own emotions, you might [6] ______________ and end the conversation suddenly because you feel upset.
- Take a deep breath when you feel [7] ______________! It's normal to feel nervous. Relaxing your mind and body can help you regain focus.
- It is a good idea to [8] ______________ some solutions to end the conflict. Take your time, don't rush. Great ideas don't appear in five minutes.
- A(n) [9] ______________ is sometimes the best way to manage a conflict. If you regret what you have done or said, it's best to admit that and say it with honesty and sincerity.
- Don't be hesitant to [10] ______________ if it's taking too long to reach an agreement. Sometimes ending the conflict is more important than getting exactly what you want.

Vocabulary practice 2

Exercise A

Read the clues and find the words.

E	W	E	M	B	A	R	R	A	S	S	W	U	C
I	M	A	R	W	V	F	E	O	A	K	I	C	O
N	G	P	H	A	P	M	S	T	T	N	A	X	M
S	B	O	A	R	W	U	P	R	O	F	I	T	M
E	U	L	N	R	Z	N	E	I	M	O	M	C	U
N	Q	O	D	F	R	D	C	I	B	M	P	U	N
S	I	G	L	P	A	O	T	U	Y	T	A	O	I
I	X	I	E	A	W	A	R	E	N	Q	C	Y	C
T	E	Z	G	S	D	J	H	S	B	X	T	C	A
I	N	E	E	S	S	I	B	L	A	M	E	C	T
V	P	A	N	I	C	M	M	P	O	L	I	T	E
E	A	W	K	V	I	O	A	Y	F	L	S	P	A
L	B	J	F	E	X	C	U	S	E	R	J	M	G
L	S	C	W	Y	R	A	C	A	D	E	M	I	C

1 Unfortunately, it is sometimes impossible to ____________ the damage that has been done.

2 It is frustrating to me that my co-workers are sometimes ____________ to my feelings.

3 I know we made a mistake, but I hope the supervisor doesn't ____________ us in front of the team.

4 The changes they have made in the structure of the company will ____________ all the employees, not just the top managers.

5 The company has to start making a(n) ____________ soon or it will have to close down.

6 Most people are now ____________ of the environmental problems that are caused by our industry.

7 I will always tell the truth and not look for a(n) ____________ if I make a mistake at work.

8 I think you can contribute a lot if you take on a more active role in the project and be less ____________.

9 I may not agree with his ideas, but I still have great ____________ for his work.

10 The secretary lost the final version of the report, so he was in a(n) ____________.

Exercise B

Use the correct words from the puzzle to complete the conversations.

1

I won't mention all his mistakes in the document because I don't want to 1 ____________ him.

That's very nice of you. Some managers can be quite 2 ____________ to their employees' feelings.

2

Do you think your manager is 3 ____________ of the problem you have with your co-worker?

Yes, but she doesn't think it is important and that we shouldn't use that as a(n) 4 ____________ not to work together.

3

Has the financial crisis had a(n) 5 ____________ on your sales this year?

Yes, this year has been difficult, but the company hopes to make more 6 ____________ next year with our new marketing strategy.

Vocabulary practice 3

Exercise (A)

Complete the puzzle. What is the vertical word?

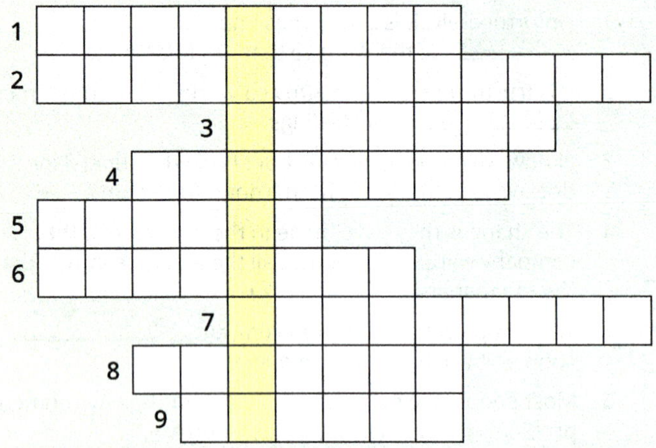

1 achieving the results that you want: *a(n)* ____________ *solution*
2 to complete what you started doing: *to* ____________ *with a plan*
3 to watch something carefully to see if it changes: *to* ____________ *something*
4 to make you remember something: *to act as a(n)* ____________ *of something*
5 when something is available for everyone to see, hear, or read: ____________ *information*
6 a detailed plan to achieve success in something: *work on a new* ____________ *to increase sales*
7 a way of doing an activity: *develop a(n)* ____________ *for getting more customers*
8 the act of looking at how something is developing: *have a regular* ____________
9 to make small changes to improve something: *to* ____________ *the volume*

Exercise (B)

Use the correct words from the puzzle to complete an employee's journal.

How to achieve my goal

1. *Write down the goal and put it somewhere I can easily see as a daily* ¹____________.
2. *Find a friend I can talk to who can help me stay* ²____________ *to my goal.*
3. *Develop a detailed* ³____________ *to help me achieve my goal.*
4. *Make a plan to have a(n)* ⁴____________ *every week to make sure that I'm on track.*
5. *Remember that I can always* ⁵____________ *my strategies if they are not working well.*

Vocabulary practice 4

Exercise A

Complete the puzzle.

Across

1 someone's job or duty

6 ready to accept or consider other ideas and points of view

8 the act of working together to achieve a goal

10 to communicate with someone or react to something

11 the position or purpose that someone or something has

12 made smaller or less than it used to be

Down

2 not enough in amount or quality

3 the quality of someone's voice that shows their emotions

4 that can be trusted

5 a strong feeling of interest and passion

7 to tell others about something important

9 not willing to make a change

10 to give someone an idea about what to do or create

Exercise B

Use the correct words from the puzzle to complete the conversations.

1

Are you excited about your new 1 __________ on this project?

Yes, I can't wait for my new position to be official. The manager is going to 2 __________ it tomorrow.

2

Teamwork is usually fun and productive, especially if you have 3 __________ co-workers who listen to new ideas.

That's right. When co-workers are 4 __________ and don't want to change, teamwork can be very challenging.

3

If we want to make the deadline, we need to work in 5 __________ with each other on the final draft of the proposal.

I agree. By working together, we can also 6 __________ each other by exchanging ideas.

4

Now that I know our competitors have bigger budgets, I have lost some of the 7 __________ I had for the project.

Yes, I can hear the frustration in your 8 __________ of voice.

Vocabulary practice 5

Exercise (A)

Read the clues and find the words.

R	C	L	C	R	E	D	E	N	T	I	A	L	S
E	O	J	D	T	I	S	O	U	R	C	E	F	J
L	U	N	E	U	T	R	A	L	V	J	W	S	G
I	R	L	R	A	R	E	P	U	T	A	B	L	E
A	S	Q	S	C	O	M	M	E	R	C	I	A	L
B	E	U	A	R	T	I	C	L	E	A	K	P	S
L	E	A	F	G	A	K	C	K	V	U	W	E	C
E	I	L	A	R	T	R	H	K	E	T	B	R	H
M	B	I	A	S	E	D	M	H	R	H	G	S	E
M	L	F	S	D	Y	L	E	S	I	O	T	O	M
X	M	I	D	O	M	A	I	N	F	R	R	N	E
C	R	E	D	I	B	L	E	X	Y	I	T	A	D
E	L	D	E	X	T	R	E	M	E	T	W	L	P
E	R	E	L	E	V	A	N	T	D	Y	N	B	D

1 This website is ______. All the information is checked by experts before being published.

2 Her story of what happened is not ______. I doubt that she is telling the truth.

3 We can use all the data they have supplied because it's all ______ to our research.

4 A conflict between two colleagues can be resolved by someone ______.

5 This is a(n) ______ institution. Our main goal is to make profit.

6 Try to listen before you react. It's easy to be ______ against her ideas.

7 The whole plan turned out to be a(n) ______ to steal the investors' money.

8 Henry has the proper ______ to be an assistant in our department.

9 Please ______ your security information when logging in.

10 I trust this insurance company because they are quite ______.

11 The supervisor has the ______ to change the deadline for the project.

12 She has a bachelor's degree in Human Resources, so she is a(n) ______ trainer.

Exercise (B)

Use the correct words from the puzzle to complete the checklist.

What to Consider When Using Sources

- *Make sure that you are using* [1] ______ *websites for your sources.*
- *Check that the person who wrote the information is* [2] ______ *in that area of work or study. Look for their qualifications and credentials.*
- *Check that the information has been published by a* [3] ______ *company or organization that is well known.*
- *Read the information and see if the tone is objective and* [4] ______*. Make sure that it doesn't rely on the author's personal opinions.*
- *Check that the information is based on facts that you can* [5] ______*.*

Vocabulary practice 6

Exercise A

Complete the puzzle. What is the vertical word?

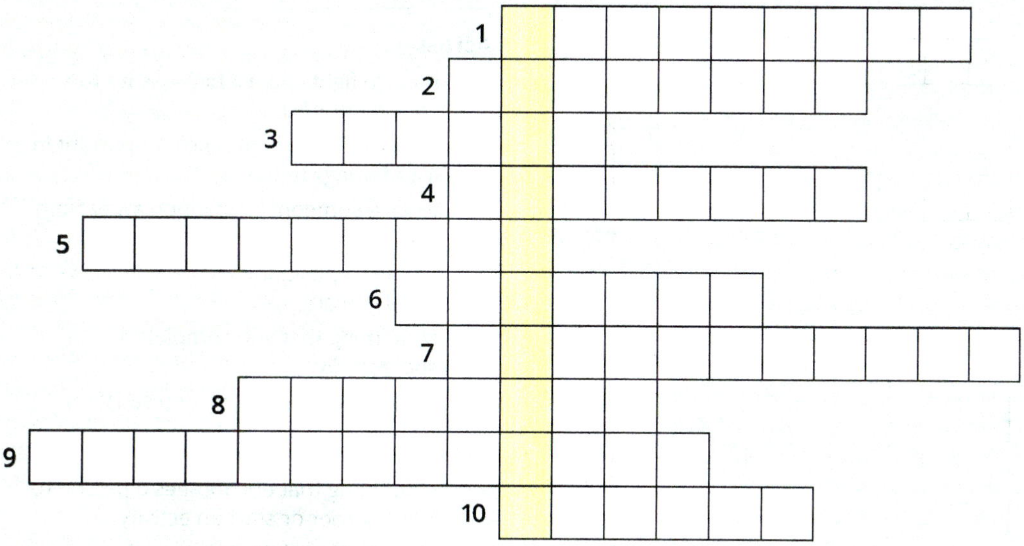

1 to work together to achieve a goal: *to* __________ *with others to get a good result*
2 to deal with a difficult situation: *to* __________ *a problem*
3 someone who gives a less experienced person advice and help: *to act as a(n)* __________
4 thinking or saying that a person or thing is bad or wrong: *be* __________ *of their plan*
5 thinking that a person or thing is special or unusually good: *be* __________ *by their hard work*
6 unsuccessful: *unfortunately, the project was a(n)* __________
7 feeling frightened, nervous, or unconfident: *feel* __________ *by her strong personality*
8 to encourage: *to* __________ *young people to dream big*
9 the ability to continue trying even when it is difficult: *to have* __________ *to reach the goal*
10 to make sure that something happens: *to* __________ *safety*

Exercise B

Use the correct words from the puzzle to complete the conversations.

1

The fear of 1 __________ can make people work too hard sometimes.

Yes, and they need to find ways to 2 __________ the stress this can cause.

2

I am very lucky to have Simone as my 3 __________ at work. She helps me a lot.

That's so nice! It is important to have someone who can 4 __________ you and point you in the right direction.

3

As the team leader, it is my job to 5 __________ the success of the campaign.

I have been very 6 __________ with your leadership. You are not afraid to take responsibility and help your team stay on track.

Vocabulary practice 7

Exercise A

Complete the puzzle.

Across

1 hard to fight against because it's too strong or difficult
5 to decide what is the most important in a list of things to do
7 to take someone's attention away from something
10 to have a position in a list that shows how good you are
11 something that you completed successfully
12 making you feel happy and satisfied

Down

2 something that encourages a person to work harder or start an activity
3 attractive and interesting
4 to understand and be able to deal with something
6 the amount of work someone has
8 to deal with a problem successfully
9 difficult to understand because it has many parts

Exercise B

Use the correct words from the puzzle to complete an employee's notes from a workshop on procrastination.

WORKSHOP NOTES – HOW TO STOP PROCRASTINATION

- *Learn to* [1] ________________*–If you have a few tasks to complete, make a list, decide what's the most urgent, and start with that.*
- *Be realistic with your time–Before you start, consider your* [2] ________________ *for the week and choose only a few tasks to complete.*
- *Focus on the task–Stay away from the things that* [3] ________________ *you. For example, don't check social media until you have finished the task.*
- *Give yourself a gift–Create a(n)* [4] ________________ *to meet the deadlines. For example, go to a nice restaurant after completing a task on time.*
- *Learn to relax–When you feel that the task is getting* [5] ________________*, take a deep breath and step away from it for 5 minutes.*
- *Think positively–Try to* [6] ________________ *your fear or doubts by reminding yourself of your biggest* [7] ________________ *so far and feel proud.*

Vocabulary practice 8

Exercise A

Read the clues and find the words.

P	F	P	R	E	S	S	U	R	E	W	J	G	P
S	J	V	C	G	X	Q	N	P	Y	Q	T	E	S
Y	M	U	E	R	I	O	J	N	I	C	O	J	R
C	B	Y	G	A	D	D	R	E	S	S	F	X	M
H	D	C	O	T	W	M	V	P	L	E	Y	L	I
O	R	A	M	I	R	G	C	O	M	M	I	T	P
L	E	N	A	T	E	Q	E	B	Z	J	W	H	B
O	A	X	N	U	C	N	A	U	S	E	O	U	S
G	L	I	A	D	O	G	K	F	G	T	K	W	U
I	I	E	G	E	G	E	T	R	I	D	O	F	P
C	S	T	E	U	N	W	O	L	B	N	F	X	N
A	T	Y	G	T	I	C	S	U	F	F	E	R	Q
L	I	B	I	V	Z	Y	E	J	U	O	V	Y	C
N	C	P	E	R	E	L	A	X	A	T	I	O	N

1. We care about the ____________, as well as the physical, well-being of our employees.
2. These days, I feel that I'm under a lot of ____________ to work longer hours to finish the project.
3. She suffers from ____________ when she has so much work to do.
4. I don't know how to express my ____________ for all your brilliant advice.
5. When we don't ____________ our problems right away, they often become worse.
6. He didn't ____________ the manager at first; he thought she was a customer.
7. Doing physical activities, such as running and swimming, can help us ____________ stress.
8. Having a hot bath when I get home from work is my favorite kind of ____________.
9. It's sometimes very difficult to ____________ to your goals and not give up.
10. Some people feel ____________ before important meetings because they get very nervous and anxious.
11. He is very ____________ about his abilities. If he can't do it, he will tell you.

Exercise B

Use the correct words from the puzzle to complete the conversations.

1

What do you do when you feel 1 ____________ about meeting deadlines at work?

I think positively, but if I get really stressed, I meditate for a few minutes at my desk for 2 ____________.

2

I need someone to help me 3 ____________ what is making me unhappy.

Yes, and then you will be able to 4 ____________ the cause and make a change.

3

I believe that Jenn can 5 ____________ to the plan and finish all her tasks by the end of the week.

I agree. It's not much time, but she works well when she's under 6 ____________.

Vocabulary practice 9

Exercise (A)

Complete the puzzle. What is the vertical word?

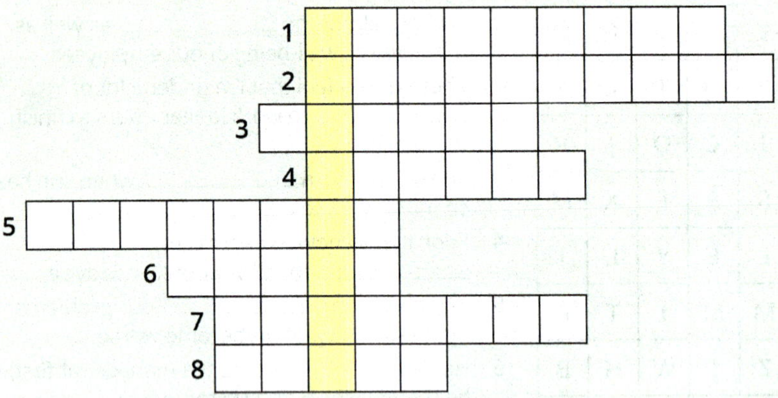

1 variety in people, ideas, or things: *ethnic and cultural* ____________

2 the act of putting money into something to make a profit: *a good* ____________

3 to judge and decide how good or bad something is: *to* ____________ *your strengths or needs*

4 to try hard to achieve something: *to* ____________ *a career in finance*

5 the production of a gas or other chemical that goes into the air: ____________ *from a factory*

6 rude or violent treatment of a person: *physical* ____________

7 something that is usually done as a habit or tradition: *common* ____________

8 to have a high opinion of something: *to* ____________ *someone's opinions*

Exercise (B)

Use the correct words from the puzzle to complete an employee's email to her manager.

Email

Vera Fern
To: Darren Miller
Subject: Reminder regarding the project

Dear Mr. Miller,

I would like to thank you again for the workshop on sustainability in the workplace. I greatly 1 ____________ what you said about the role of businesses in environmental protection. I agree that we need to first 2 ____________ our current approach before committing to a more environmentally-friendly 3 ____________ of doing business. I am really impressed by your new plan regarding waste 4 ____________. I think that building a sustainable business is an incredibly smart 5 ____________ in our company's future and that we must 6 ____________ this to help protect our environment.

I really appreciate your help! Looking forward to hearing from you!

Best,

Vera Fern

Vocabulary practice 10

Exercise A

Complete the puzzle.

Across

1 the part played to help something be successful
4 an official document that shows that someone is allowed to do a job or that something is the right quality
5 a document that lists a person's education and previous jobs and is sent to an employer
8 to make sure that everyone is working correctly
10 a quality in a person's character
12 to make something easy to notice

Down

2 a short description that states the main ideas
3 an official document from a college that lists a student's classes and grades
6 to give the main information about something but not the details
7 the process of judging the quality or importance of something
9 to be better than others in a way that is obvious
11 to connect to something else

Exercise B

Use the correct words from the puzzle to complete the conversations.

1

It's our loss that he will be leaving the team. His 1 ____________ to the project has been significant.

Yes. Now you will have to 2 ____________ the advertising team and make sure they successfully finish the project on time.

2

What do you think is the number one 3 ____________ that most employers look for in an employee?

Personally, I think candidates who are honest in the interviews will 4 ____________ from the others and get the job.

3

Jesse told me that you have been searching for a job. Do you have your 5 ____________ ready?

Yes, I made some more changes yesterday, but I still need to 6 ____________ my professional experience so I can put it in the overview.

Vocabulary practice 11

Exercise A

Read the clues and find the words.

A	C	C	W	P	Q	T	R	E	N	D	X	E	C
D	R	U	M	G	S	K	I	L	L	C	L	N	A
V	I	L	D	O	W	N	S	I	D	E	V	T	N
A	T	T	V	O	V	O	E	O	T	M	C	R	D
N	I	U	C	D	F	V	W	C	Q	X	O	Y	I
C	C	R	T	F	X	H	G	J	M	I	N	L	D
E	I	E	F	I	R	S	T	H	A	N	D	E	A
S	Z	L	Z	T	L	D	U	Z	L	L	U	V	T
W	E	N	V	Q	O	X	E	O	G	K	C	E	E
I	N	F	O	R	M	A	T	I	O	N	T	L	W
I	M	P	R	E	S	S	I	O	N	R	Q	D	V
W	E	G	F	T	H	D	J	S	E	A	R	C	H
F	I	E	L	D	L	Z	A	W	K	W	A	R	D
P	O	T	E	N	T	I	A	L	B	H	N	X	O

1 Scientists hope there will be some major ____________ in the field of medicine.

2 I never ____________ colleagues. I always find something positive.

3 If you want to make a good first ____________ in the meeting, you should try to be on time.

4 The boss will ask ____________ employees certain questions to learn more about them.

5 The salary is competitive, but the ____________ of the job is that you will have to travel a lot.

6 She didn't study it, but she has ____________ experience in business management.

7 It was really ____________ when they asked me about my personal life in the interview.

8 The latest ____________ in finding the right employee is to search on social media.

9 I believe that I am a(n) ____________ for the position based on my education and previous work experience.

10 The manager has to go to an important meeting today, I will ____________ the interview instead.

11 She just graduated from college, so she will be happy with a(n) ____________ job.

12 You need to highlight the most relevant skills in your résumé to show that you are the best ____________ for the position.

Exercise B

Use the correct words from the puzzle to complete the notes from a seminar preparing senior students for job interviews.

SEMINAR NOTES – STEPS OF AN EFFECTIVE INTERVIEW

- *Preparation: Before the interview, spend some time to learn about the company and do research on the latest* [1] ____________ *in the industry.*
- *Introduction: Make a good first* [2] ____________ *by smiling and making eye contact with the person who will* [3] ____________ *the interview.*
- *Talk about your experiences: Make sure that you don't talk negatively or* [4] ____________ *your former employers and co-workers.*
- *Answer questions: Give short and clear answers. Make sure to emphasize what makes you a(n)* [5] ____________ *for the position.*
- *Ask questions: As a(n)* [6] ____________ *employee, use this opportunity to learn about the kind of* [7] ____________ *you can make in the future.*
- *Wrap-up: End with a handshake and thank the interviewer. After the interview, ask yourself if you felt respected as a(n)* [8] ____________ *and if you successfully highlighted all of your relevant skills.*

Vocabulary practice 12

Exercise (A)

Complete the puzzle. What is the vertical word?

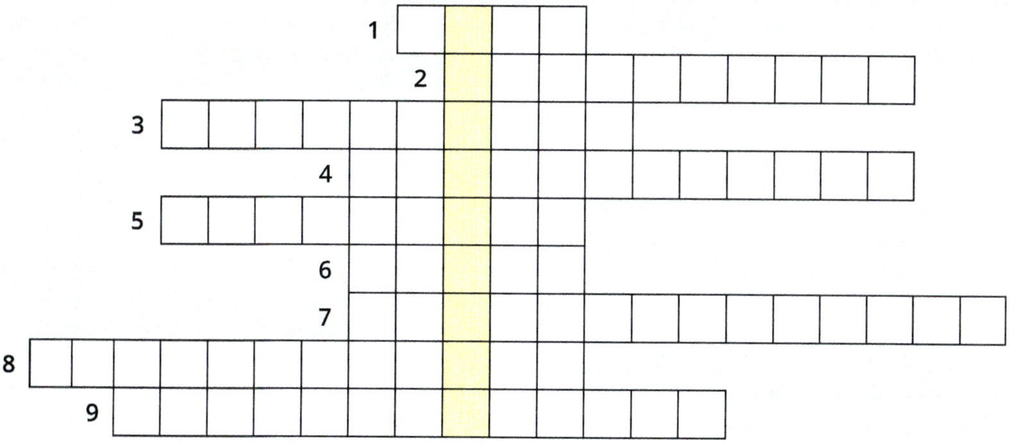

1 to be ready to deal with a difficult situation: *to* ______________ *serious problems*
2 creating a large amount of something: *a(n)* ______________ *employee*
3 to expect something: *to* ______________ *the outcome*
4 to persuade that you have a lot of ability: *to* ______________ *in a job interview*
5 the act of showing someone that they are not wanted: *a(n)* ______________ *letter*
6 to be very good at something: *to* ______________ *at math*
7 a quality of something or someone: *his best* ______________
8 a person's bad qualities or weaknesses: *to hide your* ______________
9 facts or events that make a situation the way it is: *under these* ______________

Exercise (B)

Use the correct words from the puzzle to complete the conversations.

1

I have applied to eight jobs and received eight 1 ______________ emails. Do you think I should give up?

No. Just update your résumé and learn to 2 ______________ better in interviews.

2

What do you think they will ask in the interview? I am sure there will be questions about the areas that I 3 ______________ at. I'd better prepare for those!

Yes, but they will also try to learn about your 4 ______________. So, you will need to be ready to talk about both your strengths and weaknesses.

3

I heard you had three interviewers in the meeting. Did you manage to 5 ______________ your fear of speaking to a group?

Luckily, I did some research before the interview, so I was able to 6 ______________ having more than one interviewer. I think I did well because I didn't feel very anxious.

Glossary

Module 1: Communication 1

irritating (adj) making you feel angry or annoyed
paralegal (n) someone whose job is to help a lawyer do his or her work
personality (n) someone's character and how he or she behaves toward other people

Module 2: Communication 2

abrupt (adj) speaking with few words in a way that seems rude or unfriendly
ambiguity (n) when something can have more than one possible meaning
context (n) the words that come before and after a word or phrase and help you understand its meaning
medium (n) a way of communicating information or ideas
shoot off (phr v) to write and send a brief message to someone very quickly

Module 3: Goal Setting

biochemist (n) a scientist who studies the chemical processes that take place in living things
decorate (v) to make something look more attractive by adding pretty things to it
influential (adj) having a lot of influence and therefore changing the way people think and behave
loan (n) an amount of money that you borrow, especially from a bank
recognition (n) public praise and thanks for what someone has done
supplier (n) a company that provides things for businesses to buy
up and running (phr) open and operating normally

Module 4: Teamwork

campaign (n) a series of things you do in order to persuade people to do something
credit (n) praise given to someone for doing something
criticize (v) to say that someone or something is bad
flock (n) a group of sheep, goats, or birds
in confidence* (phr) if you tell someone something in confidence, you do not want him or her to tell anyone else
off the top of your head* (phr) if you say something off the top of your head, you say it immediately, without thinking carefully or checking the facts

Module 5: Critical Thinking

citation* (n) words or lines taken from a book, play, speech, etc. by someone else, which you mention
figure (n) an important or famous person
inaccurate (adj) not completely correct
peer-reviewed* (adj) carefully examined by another scientist or expert in the same field

* in audio

Module 6: Leadership

concern (n) a feeling of worry about something important, or the fact of caring about it
performance review (n) a meeting between a worker and a manager to discuss how the worker is doing in his or her job, what might happen in the future, etc.
struggle (v) to try very hard to do or achieve something difficult
to someone's credit (phr) making someone deserve praise for doing something

Module 7: Self-Management

have all the time in the world (phr) used to say that there is a lot of time to do something
momentum (n) the ability to keep increasing, developing, or being more successful
pile up (phr v) to become larger in quantity or amount, in a way that is difficult to manage
think straight (phr) to be able to think clearly

Module 8: Wellness

Chinatown (n) an area in a city where there are Chinese restaurants, stores, and where a lot of Chinese people live
custody (n) the legal right to take care of a child
goof off (phr v) to waste time or avoid doing any work
split up (phr v) to end a marriage or relationship
takeout (adj) (of food) bought at a restaurant to be eaten at home

Module 9: Social Responsibility

agricultural (adj) relating to the activity of growing crops and raising animals for people to eat
best practice (n) procedures at work that are accepted as being the most effective
environmentally-friendly (adj) not damaging the environment
faculty (n) the teachers in a school, college, or university
low-carbon (adj) causing a small amount of carbon dioxide into the environment; using energy sources that do not harm the environment
minimum wage (n) the lowest amount of money that an employer can legally pay per hour to a worker
overstock (n) things of which you have more than you need or can sell
publicity (n) the attention that newspapers, television, or radio gives to someone or something
rack (n) a frame, bar, or shelf that things are put on
recognition (n) the act of knowing someone because you have seen him or her before
seasonal laborer (n) a worker who only works during a particular season of the year

Glossary

Module 10: Branding

brochure (n) a thin book that gives information or advertises something
campaign (n) a series of things that you do in order to persuade people to do something
graphic designer (n) someone whose job it is to draw and design, especially for magazines, advertisements, or websites
logo (n) a picture that is the official sign of a company or organization
minimal (adj) very small in amount
plus (n) something good about a situation

Module 11: Job Search

curious (adj) wanting to know or learn about something
get out of one's way (phr) to avoid interfering with what someone is doing
referral (n) an act of sending someone or something to another person or place for help, information, a decision, etc.
straightforward (adj) honest about your feelings or opinions and not hiding anything

Module 12: Interviewing

crisis (n) a bad situation with problems that must be dealt with quickly, or the situation will get much worse
innovative (adj) new and better than in the past
landscape gardening (n) the profession or art of arranging gardens and parks so that they look attractive
level-headed (adj) calm and sensible in making judgments or decisions, or showing this quality
maintenance (n) work that is done to keep something in good condition and working correctly
mentoring (n) a system of using people with a lot of experience, knowledge, etc. to advise other people and give them encouragement to succeed at school or work
passion (n) a strong feeling of liking something
varying (adj) different from other things of the same type

Notes